Heal The Body Heal The Mind

A Somatic Approach To Moving Beyond Trauma

Susanne Babbel, PhD

16pt

Copyright Page from the Original Book

Publisher's Note

This publication is designed to provide accurate and authoritative information in regard to the subject matter covered. It is sold with the understanding that the publisher is not engaged in rendering psychological, financial, legal, or other professional services. If expert assistance or counseling is needed, the services of a competent professional should be sought.

Distributed in Canada by Raincoast Books

Copyright © 2018 by Susanne Babbel
New Harbinger Publications, Inc.
5674 Shattuck Avenue
Oakland, CA 94609
www.newharbinger.com

Cover design by Amy Shoup

Acquired by Jess O'Brien

Edited by Amy Johnson

All Rights Reserved

Library of Congress Cataloging-in-Publication Data on file

TABLE OF CONTENTS

Foreword	iv
Acknowledgments	ix
Introduction	x
CHAPTER 1: Understanding Trauma	1
CHAPTER 2: How Trauma Impacts Body and Health	38
CHAPTER 3: Love after Trauma	75
CHAPTER 4: Sexual Healing	122
CHAPTER 5: Creating a Trauma-Resilient Relationship	154
CHAPTER 6: Overcoming Financial and Career Barriers	189
CHAPTER 7: Triumphing Over Disempowering Beliefs	218
CHAPTER 8: Vuja De: Finding Meaning after Trauma	253
References	271
Back Cover Material	297

"This is clearly a book that all survivors of trauma, therapists, and other mind-body healers can greatly benefit from. It is comprehensive, thoughtful, well written, and scientifically grounded. The book combines both theory and practical mind-body exercises that show how one can recognize the limiting patterns resulting from trauma. Then, most importantly, it guides the reader to create new patterns in the areas of health, love, spirituality, work, and finances. Susanne has simplified this body-based approach to trauma so readers will find it user-friendly and applicable to their particular situation."

—**Peter A. Levine, PhD,** author of *Waking the Tiger* and *In an Unspoken Voice*

"This groundbreaking book offers understanding and healing to anyone who has suffered any trauma in their lifetime. It is a source of wisdom, empowering readers to break through limitations and achieve their highest potential. I highly recommend it to all who seek greater awareness and an ever more fulfilling life."

—**Patricia Evans,** author of *The Verbally Abusive Relationship*

"In *Heal the Body, Heal the Mind,* author Susanne Babbel has done a magnificent job explaining the difficult and complex topic of trauma in terms that are easy to understand. The practical solutions she offers stand up to real-life circumstances. Well done!"

—**Suzanne Scurlock-Durana,** author of *Reclaiming Your Body* and *Full Body Presence*

"Trauma leaves its traces deep within the emotional brain, generating intrusive feelings of anxiety and helplessness. *Heal the Body, Heal the Mind* is a comprehensive, effective guidebook that takes victims of trauma along a path of deep recovery, allowing them to bring emotional, spiritual, and cognitive energy directly to the source of their wounds."

—**Susan Anderson,** author of *The Abandonment Recovery Workbook* and *Taming Your Outer Child*

"Susanne Babbel offers an admirably comprehensive, readable, and practical guide to recognizing the various forms of trauma and how to heal from it so that our lives can move forward. Through her deep insights, gentle guidance, and helpful exercises, this book offers a pathway to reconnecting with ourselves and moving toward a more joyful and meaningful life. I highly recommend this book."

—John Amodeo, PhD, author of *Dancing with Fire* and *Love and Betrayal*

Foreword

Do you think of yourself as a trauma survivor? I didn't. Yes, my childhood was filled with abuse and neglect until I ran away from home at age sixteen and lived with strangers. Even so, I would never have labeled it as "trauma." It wasn't until I was a practicing psychotherapist and professor of clinical psychology that I began my deep healing work. Through this I realized that most of my difficulties stemmed from those early traumatic experiences.

In leading retreats, workshops, and trainings all over the United States and Europe, I find we are all very similar. Regardless of our current achievements and successes, many of us lead lives of quiet desperation. We stumble from day to day coping with anxiety, depression, physical symptoms, or simply a less than fulfilling life.

The good news is, it's never too late to heal. Through her own personal and professional work, Dr. Susanne Babbel has unearthed the best processes and practices to help you actually move from where you are to where you want to be in your life. With this book, she provides a proven roadmap to lead you through your own healing journey.

I remember many years ago Susanne sitting in my office when she applied to our doctoral program in somatic and clinical psychology. As founder and president of the graduate school I met many aspiring therapists. Susanne was different. She saw beyond what was there; she always saw what was possible and moved toward it. We stayed in touch through her doctoral research and beyond as she continued to push the envelope. She was always bridging mind and body practices and garnering practical processes from the latest research. She began writing for *Psychology Today* and soon had thousands of followers who became engaged in her ideas. As they began practicing her suggested processes, many left comments about the major shifts they experienced in their lives. As a result of her research, her almost two decades of clinical practice, and her writing, this book was born.

The processes in the book parallel my own research and discoveries. I apply similar mind/body research in intensive retreats for adults to heal early trauma and learn to thrive. Until recently, trauma was not fully understood, and therefore was not effectively treated. We thought that trauma could only stem from experiences such as war or extreme violence. We now know that, while there are varying degrees of trauma, all trauma is stored in the body, often outside of conscious memory. And, it is clear that in order to heal trauma of any kind, we must involve the whole person.

Current psychotherapy and self-help books often offer coping strategies, which can help you get from day to day. There's nothing wrong with that but now there's so much more. Now you can move beyond coping to actually heal. When healing occurs, you can reach levels of resiliency and thriving you may not have thought possible. Simple strategies to help you do that are in this book.

Here Susanne clearly explains how anyone can heal the traumas that lie hidden within the mind and body. She shows how to tackle even the most difficult situations such as abuse, sexual healing, and financial and career difficulties. Also covered are the unconscious, hidden beliefs that keep us from reaching our potential.

She speaks directly to you, the reader. I felt as though I was sitting across from her in her office and she was walking me through exactly what I needed. It all seemed designed specifically for me. I can hear her say to each of us, "You are worthy, you are lovable, you deserve..."

I encourage you to begin now. Imagine what your life will be like in a few weeks when you have begun this step-wise process toward wholeness. Imagine how you will feel in a few months when you are able to be more present and go about your day feeling more calm and confident. You have in your possession an exceptional and proven guide for your journey. You have taken the first step. I am confident that

it will take you exactly where you need to go.
—Marti Glenn, PhD
Clinical Director, Ryzio Institute
Santa Barbara, CA

Acknowledgments

I want to acknowledge my great editor Kathy Glass, who has been my cheerleader and guide during the process of writing this book.

I am grateful to the New Harbinger team, including acquisition editor Jess O'Brien for reaching out to me, editors Nicola Skidmore, Clancy Drake, and Amy Johnson, and everyone else who helped make my dream of publishing this book come true.

Many thanks to all of my readers who are willing to take the risk to heal, and particularly to the readers of early drafts of this book, whose gentle feedback showed me what would be important and helpful to include.

Thank you to my family and friends, for your support and patience—and for waiting for me to complete this manuscript to socialize again.

My gratitude also goes to Michael, who has allowed me to share his story as an example of hope for other trauma survivors.

Introduction

"There came a time when the risk to remain tight in the bud was more painful than the risk it took to blossom."
—Anaïs Nin

Many people, unaware that they are living in the shadow of past trauma, wonder what is wrong with them. Though widespread, trauma and post-traumatic stress disorder (PTSD) are largely unknown or misunderstood. Sometimes people are under the impression that only war veterans and the severely abused can have trauma symptoms and PTSD. This is not true. Increasingly, the medical profession recognizes that any type of trauma can potentially affect one's psychological and physical health—and that the impact can last long after a traumatic event. If you experienced the sudden loss of a loved one, terminal illness, abuse, war, a car accident, a natural disaster like a fire or earthquake, or any other traumatic situation, you may have ongoing trauma symptoms. When you have such symptoms for more than a month, you have PTSD.

Trauma can impact anyone. In 1997, Prince Harry lost his mother Diana. It wasn't until twenty years later, after he was "very close to a complete breakdown on numerous occasions" and sought therapy that he realized he was still suffering from this traumatic loss (Rose 2017, 49). Often we try to just let go of trauma, to bury it or distract ourselves from it, and may wish to never speak of it again. Many of us don't want to deal with our memories of what happened and the pain and grief associated with them. We may think we need to be tough and not show any weakness. Unfortunately, suppressing trauma symptoms usually just increases the suffering. And it only becomes worse when others tell us that they don't want to hear about what happened, that the trauma wasn't real, doesn't matter, or occurred too long ago to still have an impact. *If only* we could bury it!

Trauma can interfere with what we see, hear, feel, and perceive to be true, and can fill us with fear. But trauma doesn't have to dominate our experience. There is a way out. I speak from both professional expertise and personal experience. To move beyond ongoing trauma symptoms, you need to address the trauma on both psychological and physiological levels. This will allow you to heal, to reconnect to yourself and others, and to regain a sense of meaning. We can surpass trauma and embrace our life's possibilities for joy and achievement.

My goal in writing this book is to help you understand trauma—both trauma's breadth and its specific forms. Further, this book is meant to teach you to recognize and reduce the ongoing imprint of trauma in your life. Step by step, this book will try to help you unmask and alleviate the fears, anxieties, emotional and physical pain, and seemingly irrational behavior that trauma has introduced into your life. By combining theory with practical exercises that focus on body-mind healing, this book can help you change the unwanted patterns of trauma and instead build constructive approaches to health, love, work, and finances.

To guide you to healing and growth in each of these areas, this book includes more than twenty body-mind exercises, with additional material available on the New Harbinger website at http://newharbinger.com/41047. The body-mind exercises of somatic psychotherapy are powerful tools for overcoming trauma because our bodies (in particular the nervous system) themselves respond to trauma, often overriding logical reasoning.

Please don't be intimidated by the words "somatic psychotherapy." Somatic psychotherapy is simply a school of psychology that incorporates the physical body into therapy. It focuses on gaining body awareness and attending to physical sensations in addition to thoughts and emotions. By learning to connect and communicate with our physical sensations, we can let go of trauma held in our bodies.

Some exercises require a pen and paper. Others require only a quiet space and the time to get to know the incredible power of your physiology and your mind.

Please, be patient with yourself: learning anything new can bring frustrations, confusion, and resistance. If you notice any of these emotions arising, try to find soothing words that will encourage you to move past the initial learning curve and fear. As you go through this process, it's important to treat yourself with self-compassion. Think of being a friend to both yourself and your fears. As you will learn throughout this book, fear isn't a nuisance but rather an important survival mechanism that motivates you to get away from trauma by going into a fight, flight, or freeze reaction. When you approach your fears in a loving way, they have a better chance of dwindling away.

I have tried to keep this book as easy as possible to read. Occasionally I'll use the technical vocabulary of psychotherapists and researchers to help deepen your understanding and enable you to do further research on the topics of greatest interest and relevance to you. If you are new to a healing journey, it is my hope that the knowledge you gain from this book will spark personal insights and support your courage in starting this journey.

If reading this book or doing its exercises stirs up intense feelings that are too hard to handle by yourself, please consider seeking support from a psychotherapist who specializes in trauma. Receiving support is not a sign of weakness. It is evidence of loving self-care and the courage to face your fears.

How This Book Started

I have been a professional psychotherapist for more than seventeen years, specializing in trauma recovery. I utilize my trauma training and experience in my practice in San Francisco as well as in my writings. Since 2009, I have been blogging for *Psychology Today,* writing posts that have attracted millions of readers. Many of these readers have helped me refine my ideas, generously sharing their thoughts and stories.

My own trauma healing journey began when I was eighteen years old and found myself plagued by unexplainable fears. I lived with a sense of impending danger and was easily startled. Terrible nightmares kept me from sleeping well. I was afraid of men, depressed, couldn't concentrate, and often felt overwhelmed. I had a number of unexplainable physical symptoms as well. Nobody, not even my therapist, told me that I was experiencing trauma symptoms. When I finally recognized this fact in a trauma workshop I attended for professional reasons, I began to ask myself many questions to understand why I reacted in certain ways. This changed my life and in many ways provided the seed for this book.

Without anonymity, I can't share some of my experiences; others, however, I can. When I was seven years old, I was hit by a motorcycle while on vacation in Denmark. In fifth and sixth grade, I was bullied and stalked. A few years later, when I was fourteen, I became conscious during an eye surgery while still paralyzed under anesthesia. As a young woman, one of my first romantic relationships became violent. Later in life, a car accident left me terrified because for a few seconds

I thought I would die. These events had ongoing impact on my life far beyond the immediate hurts of the events themselves. I needed to find ways to recover.

In a quest to understand my rollercoaster emotions and seemingly irrational ways of being, I challenged myself to look at my wounds, my past, and my pain. I read, attended workshops and lectures, worked with different psychotherapists, and consulted healers. In the process, I gained insight into some of the complex problems that affect all of us—differently, yet with threads of commonality. I found that soothing and healing are always available but can be hard to find.

Studying ways to ease my emotional pain—and wanting to help others do the same—led me to get first a master's degree and then a doctorate in psychology. As I now know, learning to recognize trauma and to adopt methods to overcome physiological responses can relieve the burden of symptoms.

From one perspective, when I look back, I see years lost to emotional pain, years that I wish I could have spent enjoying my life. But I also see that without these experiences, I would not have sought answers—and likely would not have become a psychotherapist. I would not have written this book, nor would I have the wonderful friends who enrich my life, many of whom I know from my years studying psychology. Further, I wouldn't have had the chance to meet my many brave clients who are so dear to me.

Michael: A Successful Trauma Survivor

This book addresses a range of traumatic experiences, bearing in mind that even seemingly minor traumas can be debilitating over the long term. To show this range, I present examples from many people, including myself, of how trauma can affect us. Throughout these chapters, I also weave the successful story of Michael, a multiple trauma survivor, to inspire hope.

Let me tell you a little bit about Michael, who is now in his eighties. As a child growing up during World War II, violence defined both the state of the world and Michael's own home. His alcoholic father was violent toward him and his mother, eventually abandoning the family when Michael was eleven. A babysitter sexually abused Michael and his twin sister in their own home. Later, as an adult, he lost his twin sister, adding a deep layer of grief to his life.

Learning of Michael's experiences left me distraught. However, Michael assured me that rather than seeing the experiences as dreadful, he had been able to creatively utilize his traumas. Despite Michael's painful journey, for the past forty-plus years he has shared a wonderful relationship with his third wife. His many creative talents, including writing, composing music, and playing the piano and harmonica, bring him great joy. He had two successful careers: He was a trauma surgeon until he retired in his sixties, at which point he went back to school to become a psychologist. He then worked as a psychology professor for more than twenty years. Given Michael's success and education, one might think he had a supportive upbringing. Nothing could be further from the truth. Michael has allowed me to use his story in these pages to illustrate that *your history does not have to become or remain your destiny.*

For more than half of his life, Michael was unaware of how his past experiences with trauma continued to affect him. His subconscious beliefs about relationships, combined with self-defeating behaviors, led him to two dysfunctional marriages and subsequent divorces. Like me, he was afraid of men—despite being a man himself. He initially failed in school and he questioned his faith. Once he addressed the effects of his traumatic experiences, though, Michael was able to find his true self, the love of his life, a career he was passionate about, and a new meaning in life. He is an inspiring example of someone who overcame many difficult experiences to become an accomplished, wise, happy person.

Throughout the pages of this book, I use Michael's experiences as a running thread, combined with my own experiences of trauma and recovery and the composite narratives of many clients and readers of my blog, to illustrate the many ways that trauma can strike. (Names and other personal details have been changed to maintain confidentiality.) With our stories, I want you to understand: *you are not alone.* One or more of these stories may resonate with your personal experiences, or you may know someone who has gone through something similar. Please, read gently. If at any time you feel disturbed, close the book, take a few deep breaths, and return to the present. Continue reading only after you feel centered and calm again.

CHAPTER 1

Understanding Trauma

"Trauma is not just an event that took place sometime in the past; it is also the imprint left by that experience on mind, brain, and body."
—Bessel van der Kolk

Trauma has so many facets that determining whether or not you experienced "sufficient" trauma to have an ongoing impact can sometimes seem confusing. Both in person and online, people often ask me: "Was my experience intense enough to be considered traumatic? Do I have trauma symptoms?" In this chapter, I explain in simple terms what trauma is and what type of events have the potential to be traumatic. (I include a few technical terms as well so that you can do further research if you desire.) For a rough test for trauma and/or trauma-related symptoms in your own life, compare your experiences to the checklist provided. If you find that you suffer from trauma, don't be discouraged! This book gives you many tools to address your trauma symptoms. When you know and understand how your past relates to your suffering, you can take steps to heal and move forward.

The Big Myth about Trauma

Confusion about trauma—and whether or not you have trauma symptoms—likely arises from the myth that trauma occurs only among war veterans and victims of horrific abuse. This is a limited view. Post-traumatic stress disorder (PTSD) can afflict anyone. It comes from experiencing an event as traumatic. Common events that people may experience as traumatic include, to name only a few, accidents, natural disasters, loss of loved ones, childhood or domestic abuse, or oppressive poverty.

This misunderstanding, however, is widespread. Thus, for example, commenters on my blog have remarked that until that moment they had thought PTSD was only related to the traumas of war. Even the most recent edition of the *Diagnostic and Statistical Manual of Mental Disorders* (DSM-5), the American Psychiatric Association's set of classification guidelines for mental-health professionals, opines that only events that cause "actual or threatened death, serious injury, or sexual violence" will result in PTSD (American Psychiatric Association 2013, 271).

Unfortunately, such definitions can lead us to believe that only the most horrible and life-threatening events can cause traumatic reactions and PTSD. The problem lies in the limited description: What one person experiences as a minor threat, another may experience as a significant threat. As a result, one person may develop trauma symptoms while another may not—even when they were in the exact same situation.

Research shows that whether or not a person develops PTSD has more to do with the person's ability to cope with stress than the event itself (Porges 1995; 2004; van der Kolk, McFarlane, and Weisach 1996; van der Kolk 2014). In turn, how we react depends on our constitution—including health, history, age when events occurred, and genetics—and our circumstances at the time, such as the support available from family, friends, and community.

What Is Trauma?

We all want to make sure that we have what we need to survive, now and in the future. As human beings, we have a hierarchy of basic needs. These range from physiological needs for air, water, food, sleep, shelter, and physical and emotional safety, to psychological needs to belong, to be loved, and to fully express oneself (Maslow 1943, 1954). When these basic needs are not met or are violated, we can end up traumatized and develop trauma-related symptoms. This fact partially explains why survivors of 9/11 in New York City—who were able to go to their homes immediately after the event—showed fewer PTSD symptoms than people who survived Hurricane Katrina in New Orleans but had to stay in shelters (van der Kolk 2011). The 9/11 survivors had homes to return to that offered not only basic necessities but also familiarity, reassurance, and refuge, whereas the Hurricane Katrina survivors did not.

The following section lists events that are potentially traumatic in nature, though not all are considered part of the official PTSD diagnosis. When you experience any of these events repeatedly or for an extended period of time, you may develop what is known as "complex PTSD." (This is not an official disorder; I mention it here in case you wish to read more on this topic elsewhere.)

Types of Trauma

The following list of trauma types will give you an idea of possible traumatic events that may have befallen you or someone you love and may have ongoing adverse effects to this day. Perhaps you've never associated a particular past event with current symptoms or difficulties—this list can help you make the connection now.

I've organized the trauma types into childhood trauma, relationship trauma, traumatic female experiences, sexual trauma, attacks, elder abuse, hospitalization and medical trauma, physical injuries, natural disasters, political trauma, and systematic oppression. This list is not exhaustive; you may have experienced a type of trauma not included here.

Childhood Trauma

- Birth trauma: cord around the neck, breech birth, premature, etc.
- Physical abuse
- Emotional abuse
- Neglect
- Sexual abuse/molestation/incest
- School violence/bullying by students, teachers, or staff
- Abrupt separation—for example, abduction, kidnapping, parent suicide, death of a close family member, placed in foster care or group homes, prolonged hospital stay, etc.

Relationship Trauma

- Domestic violence, including emotional, physical, sexual, or financial abuse by a partner
- Emotional manipulation such as misrepresentation, lying, slandering, and gaslighting (making someone feel as if his or her perceptions are completely off-kilter and implying the person is crazy or delusional)
- Sudden loss of a loved one, such as by suicide, murder, accident, etc.

Traumatic Female Experiences

- Trauma giving birth—for example, severe physical injuries, massive blood loss, loss of the baby, etc.
- Painful and/or invasive gynecological procedures
- Miscarriages
- Abortions

Sexual Trauma

- Being the victim of sex trafficking

- Sexual exploitation such as forced prostitution or nonconsensual pornography
- Molestation/rape/sexual assault
- Forced enemas
- Sexual harassment

Attacks

- Animal attacks
- Assaults
- Muggings/robberies
- Shootings
- Terrorism
- Stalking

Elder Abuse

- Emotional, physical, sexual, or financial abuse by a caregiver, partner, or other
- Loss of autonomy and independence
- Neglect and inadequate institutionalized care

Hospitalization and Medical Trauma

- Major or life-threatening surgeries
- Waking up during surgery

- Anaphylactic shock
- Being diagnosed with terminal illness
- Prolonged immobilization due to casts or for other reasons
- Near-death experiences

Physical Injuries

- Transportation accidents involving cars, bikes, planes, ships, etc.
- Accidental life-threatening injury; for example, being hit by a falling tree
- Frightening falls; for example, falling into an elevator shaft, construction hole, or well
- Severe accidental injury, such as being poisoned, burned, struck by lightning, or electrocuted
- Oxygen deprivation; for example, due to suffocation, choking, or drowning
- Hypothermia

Natural Disasters

- Earthquakes
- Tornados
- Hurricanes

- Floods
- Life-threatening fire

Political Trauma

- Soldiers experiencing war
- Refugees undergoing lack of food, shelter, and medical care
- Torture
- Concentration camps

Systematic Oppression

- Genocide
- Slave labor
- Discrimination based on race, gender, sexual orientation, age, beliefs, religion, or spirituality
- Never-ending poverty
- Spiritual and religious abuse (perpetrated by trusted church leaders or members or gurus)
- Ritual abuse (brainwashing and oppression as part of cult beliefs and practices)

***

A common but illogical argument holds that if there are so many situations that can cause trauma, then we ought to just accept trauma and trauma symptoms as inevitable parts of life. I've heard both nonprofessionals and professionals say, "Well, if there are *that many* situations that can cause trauma, then almost everyone has it." Professionals and insurance companies have claimed that the term "trauma" is overused. This is a strange argument—we don't apply this rationale to other areas of our lives. For instance, when we learned that most people lacked vitamin D and calcium, we sought to address those deficits by having food industries add the missing nutrients to milk and other foods. So why would we ignore trauma? Why wouldn't we want to address it everywhere we can—for example, by integrating trauma and abuse education into schools and work settings, or by providing low-cost therapy for children and adults? Insisting that we need to discount trauma creates taboos and shame around it. In contrast, when people can acknowledge and talk openly about how trauma affects their life, we can help them get more resources to heal.

What Is Childhood Abuse?

A great deal of confusion remains about abuse. Sometimes people aren't sure what abuse is and whether they have been abused or not. The following section explains childhood abuse in more depth and provides a brief list of examples that can help you check whether you experienced abuse or not. Abuse can affect both children and adults. Therefore, these lists can be applied to adults as well, but adults have different choices available and the power differentials vary.

Physical Abuse

Many children don't know they are being abused. They think they are being punished for their actions or choices, even if they can't figure out what they did wrong. Children lack the larger context to compare the abusive interactions they experience with the healthy interactions they *should* have. As one of my patients, Clarissa, once said, "I had no idea what abuse looked like, and I never thought I was abused.

You have this idea of someone who is abused, and I never thought that was me."

What is physical abuse? Definitions of physical abuse differ across both the states in the United States and the countries in the world. The Child Welfare Information Gateway, U.S. Department of Health and Human Services, describes abuse as "physical injury (ranging from minor bruises to severe fractures or death) as a result of punching, beating, kicking, biting, shaking, throwing, stabbing, choking, hitting (with a hand, stick, strap, or other object), burning, or otherwise harming a child" (quoted in Marshall 2012, 2).

Many of those who survived abuse think that they deserved to be mistreated—because they weren't obedient enough, misbehaved, or did something to "earn" it. I want to tell you: *It was not your fault! If your parents—or anyone else—hurt you, that was not okay.* Although the abuser usually frames it that way, abuse doesn't happen because *you* did something wrong. Abuse happens because abusers lack the tools to control or manage their emotions, feelings, and behaviors, or the appropriate skills to deal with a child. This can be due to their own trauma, mental illness, lack of or misleading education, poor role models, addictions, or other reasons.

Does spanking amount to child abuse? The line where discipline ends and abuse starts can be thin. People have different perceptions of abuse, as well as of physical punishment as a form of discipline. These are influenced by culture and time period. There have been times when nobody thought much about spanking children in school or at home. However, just because something is or was considered normal does not make it right. We need to evaluate what has been passed on to us by our ancestors and society to make sure it doesn't hurt anyone. Although physical punishment has been banned in 30 countries, spanking currently is not considered abuse in the United States as long as it is reasonable (Smith 2012).

According to Alan Kazdin, psychologist and author of *The Kazdin*

Method for Parenting the Defiant Child, physical punishment usually ends up crossing the line (2009, 134). Overall, physical punishment can create more problems than it solves, leading not only to physical harm, but also to aggressiveness, antisocial behavior, and psychological issues in children (Smith 2012). Parents Raising Safe Kids, a program led by Kazdin, offers assistance to parents who seek to improve their parenting skills to avoid abuse (Smith 2012); other abuse-prevention programs exist as well.

Physical abuse, *whether severe or not,* causes more than just physical pain, scars, and medical issues. Physical abuse has emotional, psychological, and physiological ramifications, and may carry long-term consequences such as PTSD (Baz and Wang 2013). The following Physical Abuse Test lists a few examples of abuse that children may suffer.

Physical Abuse Test

To help determine if you have experienced physical abuse, consider

the following examples. Please bear in mind, these are just a few examples of physical abuse that children may suffer.
- Forced "health" interventions or treatments; for example, unnecessary surgeries
- Misused pharmaceuticals, drugs, or alcohol; for example, to make children sleepy for a caregiver's benefit
- Forced ingestion; for example, cleaning substances (such as soap); poisonous substances; massive amounts of water, salt, pepper, or hot sauce
- Snacks or meals with foods that contain a child's known allergens; for example, giving children peanut butter even though consuming it causes them to get hives
- Cold or extremely hot showers as a punishment
- Intentional starvation
- Pulling hair, pinching or slapping limbs, or otherwise causing injuries or pain to any part of the body
- Invasive body restrictions such as taping of the mouth, chaining, or locking in closet

- Consistently being deprived of sleep

***

Take a break now to be gentle with yourself and let this information settle in. Consider playing some relaxing music or talking to a friend—do something that makes you feel better.

Words Can Hurt, Too: Emotional Abuse

Abuse is not restricted to injuries of the body. Some think that emotional abuse — psychological maltreatment—cannot be *that* bad. This is far from the truth. Emotional abuse is as serious as any other type of abuse and can affect adults as well as children. It includes nonphysical threats, excessive controlling behaviors, intimidation, terrorizing, and stalking; consistent belittling, blaming, shaming, and humiliating; isolation; and being extremely critical or hard to please (Marshall 2012). Emotional abuse includes being dismissed, infantilized, or bullied because of gender, race, class, looks, age, sexual orientation, beliefs, heritage, or anything else about you. Emotionally abusive behaviors strive to decrease a person's sense of self-worth, self-respect, equality, or identity.

"Verbal abuse" describes any words and phrases that *negatively* define you and your inner world, including your motives and feelings. As with emotional abuse, verbal abuse can be extremely painful, in the short term and the long term. As one of my clients who was verbally abused once remarked, "Each humiliating word felt like a fist in the stomach." Verbal abuse is different from rudeness. Being rude is based on poor manners and thoughtlessness, and involves no intention to hurt someone. In verbal abuse, words are repeatedly expressed with anger, and are meant to be painful.

The following tests can help you determine if you have been emotionally or verbally abused.

Emotional Abuse Test

Have you experienced any of the following:

- Threats of abandonment or separation
- Being continuously screamed at
- Withholding of love, affection, or attention as punishment (note: this is different from when a parent needs to take a break)
- Having your secrets exposed without your consent
- Having lies told about you to others
- Being forced to listen to threats, or to witness or hear about attempted suicides
- Being threatened with harm to you or someone else
- Being forced to harm others or animals
- Witnessing abuse of other people or animals
- Being exploited or corrupted to fulfill someone else's dream
- Being blackmailed
- Being threatened with withdrawal of financial support as punishment; for example, children in college
- Having someone wipe feces or urine or similar on you in order to induce feelings of disgust

- Isolation or confinement, such as a timeout that exceeds an age-appropriate time limit
- Being excessively controlled or monitored
- Being stalked

Verbal Abuse Test

The following list can help you determine if you have experienced the under-recognized yet harmful situation of verbal abuse.

- Repeated name-calling
- Humiliating or degrading remarks such as "whore," "stupid," "worthless," "ugly," "fat," and so on
- Purposefully embarrassing you in public
- Complaining about you to others in front of you
- Being continuously screamed at
- Using profanity such as "you bitch/asshole/fag" and so on
- Downgrading accomplishments
- Cruel and insulting comments such as "you are a rotten kid"
- Scapegoating you, such as "you are the reason why _____."

***

Please understand: *you ought to be treated with kindness; nobody should treat you as deserving less than that.*

Neglect and Not Having Enough

Abuse isn't only specific physical or emotional behaviors directed at a child or adult, it can also take the form of a lack of appropriate care. Children, for example, need to feel loved and have appropriate clothing, shelter, nutritious meals, education, and healthcare. When a caregiver doesn't provide these, the child suffers from neglect. Not having enough food can be traumatizing for anyone, child or adult. And it can have long-term physical consequences. For example, malnutrition can hinder brain development and function and cause deficiency symptoms and other health problems.

Emotional neglect occurs when parents or other caregivers consistently fail to provide love or attention or otherwise fail to support the emotional needs of a child. According to the U.S. Department of Health and Human Services, emotional neglect includes "inattention to a child's emotional needs, failure to provide psychological care, or permitting the child to use alcohol or other drugs" (2013). This may be for a number reasons. For example, a parent may be withdrawn or show little or no empathy due to suffering from depression, narcissism, trauma, addictions, or other reasons. Maybe parents are "too busy." Whatever the reason, it doesn't change the fact of neglect.

Let me remind you: *you deserve to be loved.* You deserve to have all of your needs met. You deserve to be healthy. You deserve to be educated.

Sexual Abuse

Rape, sexual assault, and incest are commonly categorized as sexual abuse. Sexual abuse also occurs when someone is exploited for sexual arousal, sexual intent, and/or sexual gratification, *even if no bodily contact is ever made,* such as taking pictures of a child for the purpose of sexual arousal. Sexual violence is not limited to interactions between adults and children. It can occur between children, and between adults, including partners.

Sexual trauma can have significant psychological impact, in terms of specific memories and reminders of the trauma (known as "associations" in psychological terminology), as well as feelings of confusion, betrayal, guilt, and shame (Finkelhor and Browne 1985). This can happen regardless of whether the trauma happened as a child or an adult. Symptoms can resurface at any time, even years later.

Sexual abuse is a crime and anyone who uses a child for their sexual desires or arousal commits a felony. Each country and state has its own laws determining when a person is developmentally ready—and legally allowed—to have sexual activities with another person. Involving a child in sexual activities before that point is a crime.

Some children who experience sexual abuse are so young that they aren't developmentally aware of what sex is.

These children often express later that they didn't know what was going on, that they just obeyed an authority figure. Children who weren't aware that they were sexually abused may remember that something felt wrong or "icky." They often are confused by what happened, because touch is supposed to feel good and adults are supposed to show them right from wrong. Children are supposed to be protected by adults. Such sexual abuse can disconnect children from their basic sense of self and their confidence to know what is good for them and what is not.

In addition to violations of consent, sexual trauma can occur when sexual areas—such as the vagina, penis, or pelvis—are violated or insensitively hurt in medical procedures, such as gynecological exams, prostate exams, enemas, surgeries, and giving birth. We may experience both the invasion of our private space and boundaries and the shock to our organs as traumatic (P. Levine 2005).

Children shouldn't have to cope with anyone harming or exploiting them.

They're neither physically nor mentally equipped to handle such situations. If you have experienced sexual abuse, please know: *you did not do anything to provoke or invite sexual abuse.* Exploitation is the fault of the perpetrator, not the victim.

Child abuse is not only committed by strangers but by parents, other relatives, and stepparents, neighbors, daycare providers, babysitters, and seemingly "respectable and trustworthy" people such as police officers, paramedics, priests and rabbis, teachers, and Boy Scout leaders. Even today, children frequently aren't believed—or the abuse isn't addressed—because an abuser is someone known. When children tell their parents that they were sexually abused by a close person or someone else, parents may respond with denial or by being incapacitated. This is harmful to the child. As one of my blog readers noted, when you're not allowed to talk about the abuse you experienced—when you're denied your own feelings—you can end up with persistent, long-term self-doubt.

It's important to point out that a child who is being abused most likely *won't* seek help or call the police. There may be many reasons for this, such as:
- The child was told not to tell anyone
- The child thinks the behavior is normal
- The child is worried the abuse would get worse
- The child wants to protect the parent/abuser
- The child doesn't want to go into foster care or a group home
- The child is too ashamed and embarrassed
- The child was told the abuse is their fault
- Child Protective Services did not previously interfere or stop the abusive behavior

Sexual Abuse Test

Sexual abuse can occur in many forms. Have you experienced any of the following?

- Received unwanted sexual comments about breasts, genitals, etc.
- Nonconsensual touch, including rubbing of breasts, genitals, etc.
- Nonconsensual pictures or videos for the arousal of another
- Forced into pornography or prostitution
- Forced to tell or listen to sexual stories
- Forced to watch masturbation or self-stimulation
- Forced to masturbate or to touch someone else
- Rape
- Nonconsensual penetration with an object
- Exposed to voyeurism or peeping
- Sexual harassment with words or behavior
- Being the victim of sex trafficking

***

Some of you may have already known that you were abused. Others may be shocked to find this out. Be kind to yourself—nurture yourself and continue to read only when you feel ready. If you need to talk to someone and don't have a close friend you're comfortable discussing this with, call a help hotline (you can find resources online) or seek out a therapist. Please make sure you take care of yourself.

If you are a parent and your child has been abused, you need to consult a mental health professional to map out a healing plan. The confidential National Child Abuse Hotline at 1-800-4AChild and other organizations can counsel and help the parents of an abused child and also help abusers who are seeking to stop their hurtful actions. Crisis counselors around the clock confidentially guide callers to organizations where they can receive support, resources, crisis intervention, education, and referrals to social services. If you suspect child abuse, call your local Child Protective Services. If you prefer, you can usually do this anonymously unless you are a mandated reporter such as a psychotherapist or teacher. Do this promptly, don't wait because you know the abuser. The longer a child has to endure abuse, the more severe the impact. Unfortunately, calling Child Protective Services may not be enough alone to stop the abuse—while working in group homes and foster agencies, I've heard many stories of CPS calls where nothing was done. We need to improve our system greatly.

Witnessing Domestic Violence

Witnessing domestic violence traumatizes children—it makes them feel not only powerless and helpless, but also guilty that they can't protect their loved ones. Witnessing domestic violence entails seeing or hearing verbal, physical, or sexual violence between parents. It can also include "being forced to spy on a parent; being made to participate in an assault; being used as a weapon or hostage; attempting to intervene in order to defend a parent and/or to stop an assault" (O'Brian et al. 2012, 96). Sometimes children have to call an ambulance, treat injuries, calm down an abuser, or help a victim escape. Often they are expected to lie about the situation to cover up the violence.

A violent home can feel confusing, chaotic, intense, unpredictable, and unsafe. Children who witness domestic violence may continually worry about when the next instance of violence will erupt. They may blame themselves for being unable to interfere. Such children may also believe the abuser and blame the abused parent for triggering the confrontation, believing that if the abused parent hadn't said or done certain things, the abuse wouldn't have happened.

Children whose parents engage in domestic violence are often isolated and lack attention. The violent parent will frequently be in a rage and occupied with controlling the environment, while the abused parent is recovering and consequently not present. Not having anyone present emotionally can lead to feelings of abandonment and to approval-seeking. Children in such families also lack role models for loving and healthy relationships.

Even when such children aren't physically or emotionally abused directly, they often suffer psychological trauma from witnessing domestic violence at home and may develop PTSD. If you were exposed to violence at home as a child, please know: *There is nothing you could have done to stop it.* There is nothing you could have done to keep the peace in your home. There is nothing you could have done to protect your parent or sibling. Nor was it your responsibility to do so—you were too young. Your parents needed professional help.

***

If you weren't aware of just what trauma was, all of this information may leave you with a heavy feeling. Some of you may have had a suspicion that you had experienced trauma in the past, but now know for sure. Some of you may have already known about the far-reaching effects of trauma, but not quite understood it. Some of you may wish you had never found out and believe you would have been fine continuing with life as you are! While you may think everything is fine right now, symptoms are likely accumulating even now, and the longer they are suppressed, the more powerful they will be when they eventually surface. I know it is difficult to think of dealing with the wounds, but healing them is worth it.

Recognizing Invisible Trauma Symptoms

When you are physically hurt, such as in an accident, you may have broken bones and cuts that need to heal. Because others can see your injuries, they can empathize with your pain. In contrast, the psychological wounds caused by traumatic experiences—emotionally or physically traumatic—are frequently invisible to the eye. As a result, even though these wounds continue to hurt, all too often they're not acknowledged or accepted by others. Family members, health professionals, and society at large can't understand why you're hurting or less than fully functional, especially if the traumatic events took place years ago. This makes receiving empathy difficult. As one reader of my blog mentioned recently, even her friends dismissed her experiences because they had happened so long ago—they basically told her to just get over them.

One of the reasons why it can be hard to recognize the effects of trauma in our own lives is that our responses often cover wounds we feel but do not see. For that reason I offer you the following list of trauma symptoms you may be experiencing.

Trauma Symptom Test

There are many symptoms of trauma, past and ongoing, and not everyone reacts the same. To determine if you suffer from trauma and invisible wounds, review this list of basic trauma symptoms. Have you experienced, or are you experiencing, any of the following?

- disturbing memories and flashbacks of the event
- nightmares or night terrors that remind you of the trauma
- insomnia
- dissociative reactions
- self-inflicted injuries and pain

- irrational fears, phobias, and behaviors
- catastrophic thinking and expecting the worst
- persistent anxiety and worry
- negative beliefs about oneself or others
- feeling disconnected or estranged
- avoidance of certain situations, places, feelings, memories, thoughts, etc.
- an emotional rollercoaster of crying, being anxious, depressed, fearful, or angry
- depression
- intense irritability and anger
- feeling numb or difficulty feeling emotions
- difficulty concentrating or remembering
- difficulty experiencing positive emotions such as joy, love, and peace
- hypervigilance, or a heightened sense of being on guard
- startling easily
- hypersensitivity
- hyperacusis, or extreme sensitivity to sound frequency and volume

- self-sabotaging behavior
- extreme guilt or shame
- feeling hopeless
- panic attacks
- lost faith
- seeking adrenaline rushes through taking risks or creating drama
- lack of trust
- withdrawal and isolation
- confusion
- chronic pain or immune disorder
- constipation or diarrhea

***

In more severe cases, trauma can lead to addictions, eating disorders, mental illness, and psychotic features such as hallucinations and hearing voices. With time and deliberate effort, mental memories of trauma may fade. Body memories, however, may still remain. Symptoms can continue to develop, even years and decades later. Again, if trauma symptoms exceed more than a few months, you may be suffering from post-traumatic stress disorder (PTSD). Such symptoms can eventually overshadow health, relationships, success, and personal growth.

Let me reassure you: trauma symptoms are not character flaws. If you've developed trauma symptoms, it means that you've survived something that was intensely frightening, painful, and/or emotionally shattering to you. And if you are still standing, you've done an excellent job of surviving and probably have many skills that you're not even aware of yet.

Conclusion: Understanding the Past and Moving Forward

To be truly and fully *you,* it's important to find out who you are separate from the effects of the trauma you've experienced. You may think and react irrationally—perhaps you're even aware of this, but don't seem able to stop it. There is a reason why you act and feel the way you do. Your feelings and thoughts may be linked to a time when you weren't equipped to understand or integrate what happened to you.

Understanding that these symptoms are part of being in survival mode can help you be more supportive toward yourself. Accepting this can also inspire you to begin your healing journey. Because it's difficult to address something you're not aware of, the first step is to practice self-awareness, to practice being a nonjudgmental observer of yourself—a practice referred to as "mindfulness." Putting yourself down will not lead to quick and easy success. In fact, it's likely to just slow your progress. Instead, try to be your own cheerleader. The following chapters offer awareness exercises to help you both cope with and change your trauma reactions.

When more people in our society recognize and understand trauma symptoms, our invisible wounds will become visible. And when they are visible, rather than continuing to be misunderstood and disparaged, they can be effectively addressed and supported. Then healing can replace the suffering from trauma.

CHAPTER 2

How Trauma Impacts Body and Health

"The body keeps the score."
—Bessel van der Kolk

Remember how, the last time you were scared, you held your breath as your heart raced and your hands became sweaty? Your mind and body react together to stress, danger, and trauma. Whether a threat is physical or emotional, our physiology—our body—helps us mobilize to either fight it or flee. And when neither of these two actions is possible, we become immobilized and freeze. These three reactions—fight, flight, and freeze—are part of a survival mode that our nervous system controls.

Our bodies can become stuck in this survival mode. Even when a trauma occurred so long ago that the brain has long since buried its memory, the body remembers. Spending extensive time in survival mode can disconnect you from your body. Further, it can produce continuous physical symptoms of stress, such as over-release of hormones, constriction of muscles, and upset stomach, among others. These, in turn, can cause chronic pain and immune disorders, compromising your health.

Just as the body creates scar tissue to protect a wound, it also creates a web of cues to try to safeguard you from future harm. When these are activated, they can set off severe involuntary physical and emotional reactions, commonly referred to as "being triggered." These automatic reactions may not always seem rational or sensible to you.

This chapter details the physiology that causes trauma-related health issues and governs seemingly irrational reactions. It provides you with exercises to help manage and tame your responses, so that you can emerge from trauma's time capsule of the past and return to the now. Without the constant stress of trauma responses on your health, you'll be able to feel safe in your body again.

In order to do this, I teach you how to communicate with your body in a language it understands. Somatic (body-mind) psychotherapy offers a foundation for the vocabulary and exercises necessary to begin your nonverbal conversation with your body. As with any new language, achieving fluency takes time and practice. It is effort well spent: these conversations will allow the body to realize that the danger is over and the provoked nervous system can now relax.

Physiology of Trauma

When Martha was twelve years old, a dog attacked her. She initially tried to run away (flight), but the dog seized her leg, so she then began trying to fight him off (fight). Eventually, the owner restrained his dog. By that point, Martha had frozen up (freeze) and couldn't walk home. As she felt no pain, she couldn't figure out why she was unable to move her legs. (Freeze mode often involves numbing of pain.) Because her body had shut down, she didn't realize that her right leg was torn in several places and needed stitches where the dog's teeth had dug into her muscles and nerves. A shutdown like this involves disconnecting the body from the here and now. How did Martha's body know to switch into the fight-flight-freeze survival mode and disconnect her from pain?

Within seconds of experiencing fear, a part of our brain called the amygdala assesses whatever threat provoked the fear. Without our conscious direction, the amygdala communicates with our body via the nervous system in order to prepare a physical response to the threat. The suddenness of most traumatic events makes the act of reasoning too slow to handle everything. Your physiology—in particular, your nervous system—overrides your thinking brain. The amygdala, located in the brain, takes over, while at the same time recording memories of emotions and behaviors for future reference.

Our understanding of the physiology behind the nervous system's fight-flight-freeze response builds on work done by Walter Cannon in the 1930s and Walter Hess and Hans Selye in the 1950s (Jacobs 2001). Let me explain briefly for those who wish to have a deeper understanding. The autonomic nervous system produces our states of both stress and relaxation. It consists of nerves that connect to the brain, spinal cord, and our organs. These create a sympathetic nervous system (SNS) and a parasympathetic nervous system (PNS). Often, the SNS and PNS work in opposition to each other. Thus, for example, while the SNS activates the body to prepare for action, the PNS slows down action for relaxation. When we are not stressed, we typically operate from the PNS, in our relaxed mode. When trauma strikes, however, we typically move to the survival mode, the SNS.

When we are in danger, our body involuntarily enters a high-arousal state, alarming the autonomic nervous system. Our SNS is then activated and all our senses—such as hearing, seeing, smelling, tasting, and kinesthetic movement—are sharpened in order to increase our information about the event and the environment around us. The body also releases the hormones adrenaline and norepinephrine. These hormones both help with alertness, so that we can act quickly, and redistribute blood flow from areas where it isn't needed, such as the skin and stomach, to those where it is, such as muscles, so that we can fight or flee. (This is why people sometimes become paler or have a "deer in the headlights" look when encountering sudden shock.) When, like Martha, we are injured, our body produces hormones such as cortisol to reduce pain and calm us down.

Unfortunately, we can become trapped in survival mode. The body may continuously ready itself for the next dangerous incident, because "it could happen again." And thus, the nervous system may set itself in a chronic hypervigilant mode. Additionally, sometimes the energy it takes to react to trauma may not be fully discharged, signaling danger and preventing the body from returning to a balanced state even when the danger is long over (P. Levine 2010). Such an imbalance is referred to as a dysregulated nervous system.

Trauma and Health

Living in chronic fight-flight-freeze mode and having an overactive sympathetic nervous system can cause all sorts of health problems. During normal states of stress, the hormones and other chemicals our body releases enhance endurance, strength, and focus. However, when constantly secreted in large amounts due to chronically being in survival mode, the same hormones can impair learning abilities, memory, physical function, and the immune system. A number of medical conditions have been linked to PTSD and its chronic stress level. These include, among others, chronic fatigue syndrome, autoimmune disorders (Boscarino 2004), fibromyalgia (Boscarino 2004; Cohen et al. 2002), multiple chemical sensitivities (Scaer 2014), thyroid abnormalities, and other hormone dysfunctions. Because the body diverts blood flow during stress from areas such as the abdomen and skin to muscles and extremities, it's also common for PTSD sufferers to develop ulcers, irritable bowel syndrome, constipation, and other gastrointestinal health issues (Boscarino 2004), as well as skin problems, elevated blood pressure (Defrin et al. 2008), and heart disease or cardiovascular disease (Boscarino 2004). Additionally, the constriction and continual tensing of muscles in survival mode can lead to chronic pain (Defrin et al. 2008).

With its nightmares and insomnia, PTSD often also inhibits restful sleep. A lack of restful sleep can in turn cause fatigue, decrease quality of life, and potentially lead to congestive heart failure and chronic depression (Katz and McHorney 2002). If you're experiencing difficulty sleeping, you may want to talk to your doctor, naturopath, or nutritionist about strategies to limit cortisol secretion and to assist worn-out adrenal glands (which affect sleep)—for example, with adrenal gland supplements. In particularly difficult cases, you may also find clinical sleep programs helpful. In my area, for example, there's the Stanford Center for Sleep Sciences. For starters, you can try my free recording called "Can't Sleep," available on New Harbinger website at http://newharbinger.com/41

047. If you have trouble with night terrors, such as screaming or suddenly cowering in the corner of the room while still in a dream state, you may want to ask your physician or psychiatrist if Prazosin, a high-blood-pressure medication, might help you control the night terrors and allow you to sleep better. It's important for the person suffering from trauma-related health issues to recognize these symptoms; physicians should screen for them, too.

In addition to physiological effects, trauma can bring about psychological changes such as anxiety, panic attacks, and depression. Trauma may also trigger unhealthy mechanisms for coping with difficult emotions, such as numbing feelings with eating, drugs, alcohol, excessive internet or social media use, and smoking—all of which can lead to addictions (Ford and Russo 2006), obesity, and eating disorders. Because people with PTSD are so often chronically overwhelmed, they may find important self-care—for example, making doctor's appointments or putting together a healthy meal plan—difficult.

This is part of a downward spiral to deteriorating health. Establishing healthy coping mechanisms as well as a regular routine that includes healthy eating, exercising, and going to bed at a consistent time can help you regain a sense of predictability.

Trauma Buttons: Associations and Triggers

When we are constantly in survival mode, our overactive fear motivates us to seek safety and to take actions that will protect us, now and in the future. Thus, for example, a war veteran may automatically jump into the bushes when he hears a car backfire, a flight response. While there's no actual threat, the body identifies the sound with a familiar one and immediately reacts. Previous experience has taught the veteran that when he hears bombs and gunshots, he must jump to safety. Now, whenever he hears a sharp, loud sound, his body overrides his knowledge of his current environment and makes him seek safety. There's no logic involved—if there were, the veteran wouldn't jump.

In survival mode, we seek clues about possible dangerous situations. As a result, our nervous system, with its past subconscious interpretations and associations, may link memories and beliefs about our traumatic experiences. Later, when a reminder comes along—also called a "trigger"—these systems may react together, causing us to re-experience many of the symptoms that accompanied the original experience. Therefore, a very strong reaction to something can be an indication of the past, rather than about what is happening in the present. Subconsciously (but not randomly), a connection or association has been made between the present and a dangerous situation of the past. For example, Michael connected sundown in the present with experiences in the past of his father returning home and abuse starting around that same time of day. Connections like these prompt the automatic survival reactions of fight, flight, and freeze, which can trigger emotions, behavior, thoughts, or sensations (Goldsmith 2015).

Your traumatic memories can be activated without your being aware of it. When you find yourself reacting disproportionally or with intensity—for example, with feelings of sudden sadness or depression, fear, anger, irritation, confusion, nightmares, or dissociation—something in the present may have cued associations to past trauma. Associations linked to the external environment, such as certain objects, times of the day, sounds (for example, a car muffler), etc., can trigger thoughts, sensations, and feelings. Reactions may be immediate or occur hours or days later.

An association is about making a connection between one experience and another. Associations can be accumulated over time or be made immediately upon occurrence of an event, especially an impactful event. The field of psychology has extensively studied how we learn and link experiences via associations.

In now-famous research, a Russian physiologist named Ivan Pavlov showed that, by repeatedly ringing a bell before giving dogs food, he could condition the dogs to associate the bell with food. From then on, the dogs involuntarily and automatically salivated upon hearing the bell alone. Pavlov's theory, called "classical conditioning" or the pairing of two stimuli (in this case, hearing the bell and tasting the food) was that frequently following them with a reward will strengthen an association (Rescorla 1967).

Unfortunately, associations aren't only made when we receive a reward. B.F. Skinner, a prominent American psychologist in the twentieth century, discovered that not only rewards but also punishment can create certain associations and behaviors. His theory is called "operant conditioning" (Skinner 1938).

You may find these theories boring or confusing. Regardless, please take away from this summary two facts: Our responses are learned, and our traumatic past can later bring out unwanted emotions, sensations, movement, and behavior. Responses are not who you are and are not always chosen by you. People or circumstances may have "taught" or conditioned you, so please do not judge yourself or others for responses that do not make sense to you.

Here are a couple examples of how associations impacted my client Anne's life and my life. Anne was in the habit of checking her door multiple times to be sure she locked it before leaving her house. Often she would arrive late to work because she kept returning to the house to check it again. Even though she knew this didn't make sense, she couldn't stop herself. While exploring the root of her compulsion, we discovered that it stemmed from when a fire in her home had surged into her bedroom when she opened her door. Anne instinctively closed the door to stall the fire and then escaped through a sliding door to the garden. Unfortunately, the fire burned down Anne's house, killing her roommate's dog. From then on Anne's subconscious associated an open door with fire coming in, and a closed door with fire being locked out and safety. As a result, this association led her to check and double-check that her door was locked closed.

I used to dissociate when I got into a conflict with my romantic partner, Johnathan. As soon as Johnathan started to raise his voice or gesture with his hands—at levels still normal for other people—I was gone. Not literally, but I would feel numb and far away. I couldn't even hear much of what he was saying. I felt out of my body, as if I were in a trance and watching myself from afar. This is a form of dissociation, akin to the helpless freeze reaction. (Dissociation ranges from spacing out and daydreaming, to being unaware of oneself or losing track of time, to a chronic state of being disconnected from a sense of self, or multiple personality disorder.) For me, the dissociation was triggered by Johnathan raising his voice and gesturing with his hands. While his behavior was normal, it provoked an intense fear reaction in me. My dissociation and reaction weren't things I either chose or knew how to stop. They happened because my nervous system hijacked my brain. This must have been extremely hard for anyone who was in a relationship with me!

Some of my former partners were shocked by my reactions and didn't know what to do. Fortunately, thanks to the work that I have done, it has now been more than a decade since my last severe dissociation—hopefully it will never return.

As these examples show, we can be triggered by almost anything: a partner's hand gesture, a tone of voice, a sound, a word, touch, action, but also things like the time of the day or year, locations (for example, being on a bridge or in an elevator), emotions, and more. Our associations cue our nervous system to dial into our specific trauma program, which then prompts thoughts and feelings that are no longer based on the here and now. Often, because we don't want to feel strong negative reactions, we try to avoid these triggers and situations. Unfortunately, avoidance doesn't always work, and once you're triggered, turning off emotional reactions can be very difficult. Don't give up—while it may take time and diligent work, you can do a great deal to reverse these reactions or learn to manage them.

As mentioned, it's not always obvious where associations come from. This is because associations are often established subconsciously, part of what makes PTSD such a difficult problem to unwind. Fortunately, you don't need to know the "why" behind associations in order to heal your trauma, although we often feel more at peace when we do. More important is to learn "what" your triggers are and how to handle them.

The following two exercises will help you learn how to recognize and manage your triggers, as well as how to soothe your nervous system out of survival mode and into a more relaxed state. Your first step is to realize that your fears, reactions, and beliefs may stem not from the present moment but from past experiences—that your nervous system is leading you to misinterpret the present moment. Over time, this realization will help keep you from attaching meaning to your reactions and from buying the illusions your trauma associations and reactions try to feed you. Note: if your triggers are too difficult to deal with on your own, please allow yourself to seek professional support to work through them, as my clients and I did.

Managing Your Buttons

1. Notice when you have an intense reaction: What triggered it? Make a list of your triggers. For example: When I saw, heard, smelled, felt, tasted _____, I felt, behaved, or reacted with _____ and my bodily sensation was _____ (this might be, for example, headache, upset stomach, etc.).
2. Investigate further: What happened leading up to the trigger? For example, I _____ was when I suddenly felt _____.
3. Ask yourself: Does any of it seem familiar? Examine the situation for similarities to past experiences. For example: When I heard that person say _____, I reacted with _____. This reminds me of when I was in _____ situation when I was _____ years old.
4. Differentiate between the present and the past: Once you have

identified your triggers and how they relate to past experiences, you can start clarifying how the current situation is different from the past. This will help you return to the present moment. For example: If you were hurt by someone in the past, what are the differences between the abuser and the person you are with now? How are *you* different today than in the past? What age were you then and what age are you now? What resources did you have then and now? What abilities do you have now that you did not have then? Take a moment to consider how these differences change your possibilities: For example, today you are an adult who is a lot wiser and has more resources than when you were younger. Today you may no longer be as dependent on people as you were when you were younger, and therefore you may be safer.

5. Distinguish between truth and fact: Triggers can produce

thoughts, feelings, and sensations that may not completely match reality. If you can, please, name what is true and what is not. For example: My fear is telling me _____, but the complete truth is _____.

***

When you are triggered, your nervous system goes into survival mode. Soothing your nervous system will help you get yourself out of survival mode. The following section offers strategies to help you practice this. Such soothing can have benefits that extend beyond the short-term and may help condition your nervous system to go into relaxed mode more easily.

Taming Your Nervous System

The nervous system is put on alert by sensations. Consequently, we can also use sensations to reverse fear reactions. Certain sounds, smells, types of touch, sights, tastes, movements, and body postures can calm and begin to correct the warning signals to your nervous system. Explore what your body likes and accepts. From the following list, pick one or several soothing strategies that appeal to you. As you find ones that work for you, continue to try new ones for additional relaxation and internal exploration. You can think of these practices in various ways: as intentional, enjoyable everyday activities; as exercises to discipline your nervous system and anxious mind; and as emergency responses. Calming your body means calming your mind.

Breathing

Slowing down your breath and breathing deeply will lower your blood pressure and heart rate, helping to calm and relax you. Online, you can find many breathing instruction videos. Experiment to find one that speaks to you. I like the breathing techniques from Gay and Katie Hendricks, such as "Lifestream Breathing," in which they direct you to make a C-shaped movement with the body while breathing in and out. This C-shape gives the body the support it needs to breathe naturally, allowing you to participate fully in a relaxed way and to avoid tension and stress in the body. The Hendricks also describe a second type of breath called "Centering Breath," which involves pausing for 10–30 seconds between breathing in and out, which helps you feel more centered and less anxious (Hendricks and Hendricks 1991).

Some of my clients, such as women who experienced trauma while giving birth, associate breathing with trauma. If you don't find breathing comforting, explore some of the other strategies offered here. As with any suggestion, take what works for you and leave what does not.

Listening to or Playing Music

Music can have a powerful effect, calming your body and mind. Some websites and smartphone applications offer music and sounds specifically designed for individuals with PTSD. (Please search online for current products.) You can also simply listen to whatever songs you enjoy or, even better, songs that represent how you want to feel.

Michael, who plays the piano, discovered long ago that music not only helped him soothe himself, it also helped him articulate his trauma. "It expresses that stuff," he told me, "and so, you know, it [the soothing and renewal] comes out in my music—people love my music, even though it's relatively simple."

Singing or Humming

Singing is a powerful way to release emotions and uncover hidden feelings. Often people will sing together to express themselves, to motivate themselves and others, and to feel a sense of belonging. Soldiers sing while marching, fans sing to support their sports teams. People sing in church and by the campfire. Singing, with or without someone else, can be very powerful, in part due to the concentration and focus it demands, in part due to the breathing that supports it. According to Herbert Benson (2000) at the Benson-Henry Institute, one of the reasons singing or chanting can elicit a relaxation response is because we typically breathe more deeply when we do it. You may want to explore joining a choir or band. Alternatively, casual singing, chanting, or even humming can be very helpful. Don't hold back when you feel the desire to sing out!

Movement

Move the body, move the energy. Even just wiggling your fingers or toes or moving your eyeballs around can be helpful because it tells your body that you're not in survival mode. Try to find a type of exercise or movement that makes you feel good. One option can be trauma-sensitive yoga, developed by David Emerson at Bessel van der Kolk's trauma center and now taught in many cities. Whatever movement you choose, you don't have to do it every day or for hours on end—even just a 30-minute or shorter walk can help.

Smelling a Beautiful Scent

Aromatherapy can help lift our mood and spirit. We have both an emotional and physical response to chemicals called terpenes, and they have been scientifically proven to have specific, often beneficial effects on our physiology. An aroma that reminds you of something positive and triggers positive feelings in the brain can have a very calming effect. Try to have a favorite aroma accessible at all times—for example, by carrying a tea bag, hand lotion, essential oils, incense, or whatever suits you. One male client of mine always carries a small perfume bottle with his favorite incense; whenever he feels rattled, he inhales its scent and feels more at ease.

Tasting Something

Tasting something, such as sipping your favorite cup of tea, drinking water, chewing gum, or eating a special meal, can be calming as well. However, try to avoid emotional eating or numbing your feelings with food.

Receiving Touch

Appropriate touch releases the hormone oxytocin and relaxes the body. Getting a massage, being hugged, holding hands, stroking a pet, or wrapping up in a weighted blanket (used for anxiety or PTSD) can comfort and relax the body. Another form of touch that can be soothing is the sensation of water on your skin when you're soaking in a bathtub or a float tank. (If you're experiencing chronic pain, adding Epsom salts to the water can be especially helpful.) If you are sensitive to touch, make sure you pick something that fits your comfort level.

Pleasing Your Eyes

A funny movie, a book, or simply beautiful pictures can bring about relaxation. Download pictures of whatever soothes you onto your phone or computer. One client kept an image of her husband's hands on her phone because looking at them made her feel protected. Visualization exercises can also help reduce stress and activate the body's natural relaxation response. You can find many guided visualizations practices on YouTube—search using keywords such as "relax mind and body," "guided visualization," "meditation," "stress relief," and so on.

There are many other ways to soothe your nervous system, such as speaking, laughing, or anything else that has to do with the face. Why is that? We have a cranial nerve—called the vagus nerve—that winds from the brain and face to the abdomen and interfaces with the parasympathetic nervous system. According to the relatively new Polyvagal Theory, stimulating the vagus can calm and relax you (Porges 2004). You can also try meditation, acupuncture, and other techniques. For many of us, being in nature can help us "ground" or feel part of the web of life. There's good reason so much of our poetry, literature, and music extols the peaceful capacity of oceans, forests, flowers—and even beautiful austere deserts!

Body Conversations

Traumatic events of any type prompt not only an immediate reaction but the establishment of a trauma memory in your body, to better equip you in the future. It's important to locate the memories that no longer serve you and release them from your body. In addition, because trauma can disconnect you from your body, creating a somewhat numb feeling, it is essential to reconnect with and start communicating with your body—to have what I call "body conversations." We can access and address trauma memories via nonverbal communication, using the body's own vocabulary of physiology and sensations.

Dominant Western culture focuses more on the brain and mental abilities than on the body. As a result, many people—including both clients and psychotherapists—haven't learned the language to describe their sensations. For some, attending to their body may seem foreign. However, as trauma specialist Peter Levine explains, we need to have body awareness "to harness the instincts necessary to heal trauma" (1997, 68).

Somatic psychology endeavors to understand the connection of the body and the psyche—and to provide exercises and vocabulary to describe and deepen that connection. The word "somatic" means "bodily." As movement therapist Thomas Hanna explains, "Somatics is the field that studies the soma: namely, the body as perceived from within by first-person perception" (2003, 50). Pioneering influences on somatic psychology include Wilhelm Reich's idea of muscular armor and Elsa Gindler's sensory awareness approach (Weaver 2004). Today, the field includes many variations, such as Somatic Experiencing (SE), Gestalt therapy, Hakomi, Focusing, Keleman, Integrative Body Psychotherapy (IBP), Neuro Linguistic Programming (NLP), Dance/movement therapy, Feldenkrais, Alexander Lowen technique, and more. I apply some of these approaches in the exercises of this book.

While your psyche gives and receives information via the language of words, your body does so via the language of sensations. Eugene Gendlin, a psychologist who researched how to change thoughts and emotions held in the body, coined the term "felt sense" to refer to the act of paying attention to one's physical feelings and the story the body tells nonverbally. Sensations—and the felt sense—are part of the vocabulary that our nervous system understands. There is no need to analyze what you feel when simply letting the body communicate (for example, noticing if there is tension).

To bring about greater body awareness, a therapist might ask you (or you can ask yourself), "How do you know you are sad? When you scan your body, what do you become aware of? Which bodily sensations indicate that you are sad?" People with minimal body awareness can begin with even simpler questions—for example, "What is the room temperature?" (Rothschild 2000, 103).

Often when I ask my clients what they sense in their body, they describe their emotions. Focusing on physical sensations and the felt sense is different. And it can be difficult, because

PTSD can make us feel disconnected from our body and constantly on alert. Remember: You are learning a new language. Try to put on your curiosity hat and be patient with this new process.

So what are sensations? Our most obvious senses are touch, smell, sight, taste, and sound. We can describe internal sensations further with details about their shape, size, color, texture, weight, temperature, intensity, movement, and more. For example, does your sadness cause any constriction in your throat or anywhere else? Is your tension covering a large or small area? Because we're not used to perceiving this way, exploring these details can feel strange, silly, and very challenging. However, just as our psyche needs to process its experiences and tell its stories, so too does our body. Body awareness and body conversations allow you to address your nervous system, so that you don't have to remain on automatic pilot or in survival mode. They let you assess whether your fears are based in present reality or past experiences as well as what assumptions you're making. Important to this process is learning to regulate your sensations—that is, to accept, tolerate, and manage them. Regulating your sensations can reduce seemingly erratic reactions and behaviors and help you feel safe again.

Please don't force or push anything. Listen by observing, without criticizing yourself. Sometimes sensations will surface after a few seconds or minutes, sometimes it can take a few times sitting with your feelings before you notice anything. This doesn't mean nothing is happening, it just means that your body and psyche need time to get acquainted. Your attempts can range from feeling like nothing to being overwhelming. The felt sense makes contact with our nonverbal memories and awakens parts of the body that may have been disconnected and shut down. Please be patient with yourself. As Peter Levine notes, once you become aware of internal sensations, these usually transform into different sensations, "usually moving in the direction of a free flow of energy and vitality" (1997, 82).

Awareness of body sensations can both help anchor you in the present and help you separate past from present. You're less likely to stay lost in the past when you're aware of your current body sensations. As Bessel van der Kolk explains, an important aspect of PTSD treatment is to stay in the present, "without feeling or behaving according to irrelevant demands belonging to the past. Psychologically, this means that traumatic experiences need to be located in time and place and distinguished from current reality" (2014, 254).

The following exercise can help you stay in the present and calm down your nervous system and emotions. This is a modified version of an exercise I learned in Peter Levine's three-year trauma training program. While studying animals in the wild for trauma symptoms (through, for example, their responses to being chased by predators), Levine (1997) noticed that once a traumatic event had concluded, animals first looked around to orient themselves and then shook off the trauma in a physical manner. Orienting yourself to your environment and knowing your surroundings is a tool we can use to stay in the present and not be caught in the past. Orienting yourself to your surroundings can also help you feel safer—provided you are in a safe environment—and calmer. If you are not in a safe environment, pausing can allow you to determine the next course of action to evade a threat. Orienting yourself can be done anywhere, at any time.

Staying in the Now

1. Look around and notice what is soothing and comforting to you. This might be a plant, the books on your shelves, a candle, a picture on the wall, a tree out the window, or something else. Where does your gaze stop? If it seems odd to you that looking at a certain object brings you a sense of calmness, please just go with your feelings. This is not the time to judge or analyze yourself. I've had clients find a wide range of things comforting in my office,

including a plug in a wall outlet, the tile over my fireplace, the built-in wooden shelves, or the peacock feathers in my vase. Please see this exercise as an exploration.

2. Stay with an object you find calming for a moment and describe what you see out loud or in silence. What colors, shapes, dimensions, or anything else do you see?

3. As you look at the object, begin to attend to what you feel emotionally. Ask yourself what it is about the object that makes you feel good. For example, does a plant perhaps remind you of nature? Do you find an object's color or shape comforting? Something else? If a negative emotion rises to the surface, choose another object until you find one that evokes positive feelings.

4. Scan your body and notice where you feel the sensation of being more relaxed. Has your chest become less tight, more

expansive, and warm? Have your shoulders dropped down? How do you know that you are relaxed? What do the sensations tell you? (If this is too hard in the beginning, focus on feeling the seat underneath and behind you or your feet on the floor; try to describe those sensations.) As you pay attention to your sensations, follow them until they shift and change to a calmer state.

***

This quick and simple technique can aid you if uncomfortable or painful feelings arise while you read this book. You can also always take a break and continue reading a little later when you feel that you can absorb more information. Please pace yourself according to your needs so that you do not become overwhelmed. Recalling trauma and fears can be disturbing, even when you're working to heal. Take your time and be clear on your intent to understand yourself as well as possible.

Conclusion: Intervening with Somatic Psychotherapy

Unresolved trauma can create a circuit of physical and emotional reactions that keeps replaying while disconnecting us from our body and, at times, the surrounding reality. Research has shown that body-oriented psychotherapy interventions are well suited for people with PTSD (Price et al. 2007), because they can break the repetition cycle, reconnect us with our body, and bring us back into the current time. The exercises in this chapter help you learn to converse in a language the body understands. This is the beginning of a journey of listening, observing, and conversing with your body, the beginning of understanding and changing your reactions to improve your health, feelings, and behaviors.

CHAPTER 3

Love after Trauma

"Your task is not to seek love, but merely to seek and find all the barriers within yourself that you have built against it."

—Rumi

This chapter begins by discussing what a healthy love relationship looks like. After traumatic events, some trauma survivors have trouble remembering what healthy love relationships feel like. Some trauma survivors have never been in a healthy love relationship or didn't have one modeled during their childhood. Further, as a trauma survivor, romantic relationships can seem challenging, as you may anticipate that you will be abandoned, smothered, or otherwise hurt. In this chapter, I show you how these present feelings may have been influenced by trauma during childhood that was shaken up in adulthood, and offer exercises to help you get back on track.

Because trauma symptoms like disconnection, withdrawal, depression, and anxiety can interfere in relationships and lead you to close your heart, this chapter features an exercise to open your heart and let love enter your life. Connecting with your feelings can help you both rebuild emotional intimacy with a partner and prepare you to be in a close relationship. The next two chapters extend this exploration of trauma's effects on our love lives: chapter 4 addresses physical intimacy issues that can arrive after trauma, while chapter 5 discusses how to make or keep a relationship trauma-resilient, with advice on how to build a foundation for healthy relationships despite past experiences.

What a Healthy Relationship Looks Like

Knowing what a secure and healthy relationship looks like offers you both a useful understanding of what to work toward and a way to receive validation once you've arrived.

First of all, a healthy relationship never involves having to abandon friends, family, personal goals, or self-respect in order to please your partner. In a healthy relationship, you'll experience the following:
- Love is mutually expressed and reciprocated.
- You both respect each other.
- You both find a comfortable balance between closeness and being alone.
- The two of you trust and feel trustworthy of each other.
- You both accept minor shortcomings.
- Both of you share your emotions.
- Both of you are at ease with your committed relationship.
- Neither of you avoids conflicts.
- Neither of you reacts defensively to constructive criticism, and problems are solved with minor tension or none at all.
- You're open to communicating feelings and listening empathetically to each other's issues.
- You respect differences in each other.

- You are both able to reasonably compromise.
- You help each other to accomplish goals.
- Both of you give and receive appropriate touch and affection.
- You both share responsibilities, hobbies, and friends but also maintain your own.
- Both of you feel close to each other.
- The two of you know that there can be times when you feel more or less in love.

Relational Trauma Blueprint

Feeling loved starts with our earliest bonding experience—as early as the womb—not with our first romantic relationships as an adult. We all grow up wanting to be loved unconditionally and to know that we are lovable. We all desire to open our heart to people who are important to us, such as parents, caregivers, family members, and others, even if it makes us vulnerable in some ways.

For many years, the official view of the medical community was that while in the womb babies weren't aware of the outside world. However, researchers in prenatal and perinatal psychology such as Ludwig Janus (1997) and David Barnes Chamberlain (1988) have found that at a certain stage of gestation, fetuses connect to their parents and the world around them through their senses. They hear parents' voices and different tones, and feel the constriction of the mother's body when she is stressed. A baby in utero can smell the mother through the amniotic fluids, so that it can recognize her when born, even though its eyes cannot. A fetus is exposed to the mother's happy hormones as well as the anxiety and stress hormones typically released in traumatic events (Northrup 2005). At a certain stage, a fetus has consciousness, reflexes, memory, dreams, tastes, and the capacity to learn (Gonzalez-Gonzalez et al. 2006). People under hypnosis have revealed memories of being in their mother's womb, suggesting that babies are sensitive to thoughts and feelings and to stress in utero (Cheek

1986). A baby in utero may even be aware of factors such as if it is wanted or not, if the parents feel bonded with the baby, or if the mother feels disengaged due to her struggles such as stress or trauma during pregnancy. Your first experience of connecting and feeling loved by your parents starts in the womb and continues through childhood.

Our ability to bond solidifies with our parents or primary caregivers after birth and during childhood. Feeling safe to receive and give love, to bond and feel closeness, can be interrupted by trauma. This can happen, for example, when you open up your heart but are abused, or when you are separated from a deeply loved caregiver due to death, physical or mental illness, abandonment, natural disaster, fleeing a war-torn region, or other reasons. How safe you felt as a child to love and bond with the special people in your life laid the foundation for how you perceive the safety of connecting as a youth and an adult. Our parents are our first love. (Obviously I don't mean romantic love.) Our relationships with other close family members, including brothers, sisters, cousins, and grandparents—as well as other caregivers, such as nannies and teachers—further inform our experience of love. Our later friendships and romantic young-adult relationships build on the foundation of these experiences.

The relationship between trauma and bonding difficulty in children was first identified by psychiatrist John Bowlby (1951, 1960, 1969), while studying orphans after World War II. Building on that work, developmental psychologist Mary Ainsworth found a variety of types of bonding difficulties. Closer investigation showed that a quality parent-child bond (often referred to as a "secure attachment") can contribute to close relationships as an adult (Ainsworth and Bowlby 1965; Ainsworth et al. 2015).

A healthy parent-child bond draws on verbal and nonverbal communication, with the parent attending to the child's emotional needs for love and empathy as well as structure and consistency; being in tune with and understanding how the child is feeling (with or without words); being compassionate; and consoling a child when the child is scared (Arnett 2010). Being understood and taken care of emotionally and physically forms a sense of safety and a bond; this provides a foundation for meaningful relationship.

When we have good relationship experiences and everything goes mostly right, we end up feeling comfortable with intimacy, loved, and warm and loving toward others. When things don't go well—when we don't feel safe or a parent is too inconsistent—we may no longer depend on the caregiver to protect us and may have difficulties in the future bonding with others. Such difficulties in bonding are known as "insecure attachment." There are two types of insecure attachment: avoidant and anxious.

In general, our personalities are subject to cultural and societal influences. For example, hugging is common in some cultures; in my native German culture, it is common to shake hands. As a result, everyone ends up situated somewhere on a spectrum of distant to cuddly (Schaffer and Emerson 1964). In this book, I focus not on differences in ease with intimacy that fall within the normal cultural spectrum, but on traumatic sources of bonding difficulty that individuals may encounter. Insecure attachment due to childhood trauma can have a deep impact on how we experience love, whom we love, and whom we choose to be with later in life.

Many of my clients, as well as the readers of my blog, attest to the influence of early attachments. Michael can testify to that as well. As a child, he had no role models for a loving relationship and didn't know what unconditional love could feel like. He told me, "When I first dated and entered relationships with women, they were very, very shallow because I had no idea whatsoever what an ideal relationship might look like." Before he met his current wife, Michael had trouble being in romantic relationships and had divorced twice. Michael's upbringing led him to develop an insecure attachment, specifically an avoidant attachment. As a result, he found it difficult to form strong, deep relationships until he worked on himself and met his third wife.

Whether one is anxious or avoidant, the slightest hint of not feeling safe can activate the brain to go into "attachment survival mode" (Siegel 2011). A person with insecure attachment really doesn't want to get hurt again and cannot calm down until a relationship feels safe. For anxious people, security is established through a partner's presence and reassurance. This helps their thoughts quiet down. Avoidant people, on the other hand, feel safe in a relationship when nobody depends on them. When an anxious or avoidant person's needs aren't met, their thoughts and behaviors intensify, and they may act out more.

The good news is that, while our parents may impact how we connect as adults, we can change the way we bond, and we can develop beyond our current insecure attachment style, whether it is anxious or avoidant (Siegel 2011; Davila, Burge, and Hammen 1997). We can see this, for example, in Michael's life and his final successful marriage. Although his traumatic upbringing caused him to have an insecure attachment style for many years, his relationship attachment is now "secure." As I have seen in people I know personally and in my practice, we can change the way we love and react. It takes work to develop a secure attachment, but it's worth it.

Regardless of the specifics of the traumatic relationships we experienced as a child or adult, our important and life-affirming task is to recognize how that trauma impacted us. This will help us enhance our ability to love ourselves and others in a healthy way. To do so, we need to look at how we were loved and what areas could benefit from healing. This can be a challenging task. My client Katherine was afraid that if she looked too hard at the mistakes her parents had made she would stop loving them. I reassured her that, while she might feel angry with them at first, she could both hold them with love in one hand and look at how they shaped her life in the other.

Use the following relationship attachment test (inspired by A. Levine and Heller 2011), to determine if you are an avoidant type. You'll find a brief explanation of the anxious attachment type and a related quiz immediately after it.

Fear of Getting Too Close: Avoidant Attachment Quiz

Do you tend to be analytical, spend a great deal of time in your head, and value independence? According to Siegel and Solomon (2003), this can indicate a tendency toward avoidant attachment when combined with one or more of the following traits:

- Do you tend to feel that others are too needy?
- Are you resistant to supporting your partner during stressful times?
- Do you often work overtime, fear losing autonomy in relationships, and therefore avoid closeness?
- Do you keep love at arm's length? For example, would you agree with the statements, "I don't need someone attached to my hip," or "I'd rather be alone than have to always tell someone where I'm going?"

- Are you overly critical of your partner? Do you have a hard time accepting flaws?
- Do you criticize to disconnect and avoid intimacy? According to Siegel and Solomon (2003), this type of criticism can sometimes lead to emotionally or physically abusive behavior.
- Do you become agitated when others express their emotions? Are you likely to tell your partner or others to work on not having their feelings?
- Do you prefer to do your own thing rather than spend time with your partner? Do you spend a lot of time on your hobbies?
- Do you desire minimal or no sex and have a hard time saying, "I love you?"
- Are you defensive when you are needed or when requests are made?
- Do you experience difficulty with behaviors that could lead to a stronger connection, such as being vulnerable, communicating, acting reliably, or spending time together?

Even if you don't have all of these symptoms, having just some can make it worth looking more deeply into whether or not you have an avoidant attachment style.

***

Robert came to me after he noticed that he was constantly finding reasons to criticize his girlfriend and was feeling uncomfortable with closeness. Like anyone else, he wanted to find love, but his past had created obstacles. As a child, his severely depressed mother would threaten to commit suicide, especially when he misbehaved or she felt overwhelmed with her life. This threat is a type of emotional abuse. His mother was also very dependent on him emotionally, and Robert effectively became her substitute husband. As a result, she wasn't in tune with him and couldn't meet his emotional needs. As an adult, because he wanted distance from his mother, Robert repeated this pattern in his relationships. In therapy, he noticed that one way he subconsciously distanced himself was to find flaws with the woman he was dating, such as her wrinkles, weight, clothes, or behavior. Now, after working on this issue, he has been in a relationship with a woman for almost two years; he no longer feels he needs to criticize a partner to create distance.

When one or both parents are cold, neglectful, emotionally distant, abusive, unavailable, not in tune with, and/or not meeting the child's needs, children become emotionally distant and demonstrate the avoidant attachment style (Hazan and Shaver 1987; Siegel and Solomon 2003). This can then carry over to adult relationships. Generally, avoidant people don't think that the way they bonded as a child was important and may even report that their childhood was great. They may remember their parents enrolling them in lots of afterschool activities, but have memory gaps when it comes to specific interactions. Because as children they adapted to frustrations by giving up needs that were never met, they may have minimized their expectations of intimacy.

Fear of Being Abandoned: Anxious Attachment Quiz

This quiz will help you determine if you have an anxious attachment style (you don't need to exhibit every one of these potential symptoms):

- Do you keep track of how often your partner texts, calls, or says "I love you?"
- When you love someone, are you afraid that person won't love you back or want to be around you anymore?
- Do you feel underappreciated or not valued enough or view yourself negatively?
- Do you easily interpret another person's actions as rejection or wanting to end a relationship, even though evidence suggests otherwise?
- When your pets don't behave as usual, do you begin to fear that they don't love you anymore?
- Do you have a tendency to make excuses for your partner even when it's unnecessary?

- Are you sensitive to emotional expressions of others? Do you misinterpret expressions easily and become distressed?
- Are you afraid to break up with your partner even though you know you should?
- Do you believe that your mate could change and be wonderful one day? Or, perhaps, that it is too hard to find someone new?

***

My client Laura has an anxious attachment style that stems from her childhood. After her father left, she had an abusive stepfather. Looking back at her adult relationships, she sees that she didn't stand up for herself enough. There were intolerable factors from the very beginning of her relationship with her significant other. Because of her past, she craved love so much that her need to be loved overrode her need to take care of herself. As a result, she tolerated things in her relationship that were not okay.

For Laura, fear of the pain of losing somebody was greater than the pain she was experiencing in her unhealthy relationship. In therapy she came to realize this was problematic—and that she could change this pattern. She told me, "You don't realize that this pain is going to end up outweighing the pain of loss. You can't do it that way. You've got to go deal with it, you know?"

Many people ask themselves why they stayed in their dysfunctional relationship for so long and feel "stupid" that they didn't leave sooner. Please know: Who you pick as a mate and whether you stay or leave a relationship don't reflect how smart you are. Rather, these decisions can reveal how you were loved as a child—how your parents bonded with you—and show you what healing still has to occur. Putting yourself down for being with the wrong person isn't helpful. Instead, try to take a more compassionate approach, such as, "I don't know why I didn't leave earlier, but I will find out how to prevent repeating this mistake." Or you could say to yourself, "I still needed to heal from my past." These are just suggestions—I invite you to find statements that you relate to and aren't critical of yourself.

When children experience the behavior and love of their caregivers as inconsistent and unpredictable—in response to, for example, changes of caregivers due to divorce, illness, death, or adoption; frequent changes such as nannies, preschool teachers, foster care, orphanages, or group homes; or even frequent moves—children may become clingy and develop an anxious attachment (Aronson, Wilson, and Akert 2011). As adults, people with an anxious attachment style seek unusual amounts of contact and reassurance. They only calm when they feel their love is safe and their partner is there for them (Levine and Heller 2011).

People with an anxious attachment style can be fine partnering with someone who has a secure attachment. With someone who is not available, avoidant, or acts irrational, however, they may feel as if they are going crazy. When they are with someone who is supportive and emotionally intimate, the feeling of craziness will most likely subside. Unfortunately, because anxious people put up with a lot, they often end up with unavailable people (these are different from abusive people). This may confirm their subconscious beliefs about relationships and lead them to re-enact their past in terms of feeling alone and becoming needy. In contrast, the avoidant person gets confirmation that independence is the best answer (Pietromonaco and Carnelley 1994, in Levine and Heller 2011).

Like a Moth to the Flame

How deeply ingrained such trauma symptoms are depends on how young you were and how frightening your childhood experiences were. Some people know only love that is abusive. Unfortunately, because that's what is familiar, they may seek the same type of connection as an adult. Our first encounter with love can shape how we relate to love now—for example, it may create barriers that we aren't even aware of. Someone who was hurt in the past, whether during childhood or adulthood, won't want to get hurt again. This very reasonable resolve can, however, involve walking away from an experience with beliefs that persist long beyond their usefulness—that is, beliefs that hinder rather than serve the present moment. In working through how her experience with her abusive father affected her current relationships, my client Mindy said, "I keep seeing you, Dad—wherever I go. Different faces, different names, and I never think it is you at first. But then behind these faces it is always you. I know I must look for who is not familiar to me, so I know it is not you."

Working with clients, I've found that some women and men who have been traumatized enter relationships with the unconscious plea of, "Please don't hurt me." From a psychological point of view, this refers unconsciously to their earlier trauma. It's saying, "Please don't hurt me *again*." Some individuals may need psychotherapy to recognize their unconscious urge to seek, like a moth to the flame, the same kind of personality that traumatized them previously.

It's important to look at how we were loved, how we love now, and how people love and loved each other around us. By increasing awareness and identifying our patterns, we can discern if they began in childhood, adulthood, or after our traumatic experience and actively reconstruct the way we show love to others and how we feel loved (Levine and Heller 2011).

Some individuals seem drawn to people with particular—familiar—characteristics that aren't healthy. It's important to identify undesirable traits early in a relationship (see the following section on warning signals) and to be prepared to remove yourself from the relationship before it becomes negative or destructive. This, of course, requires first bringing the unconscious desire into consciousness, so that you know what you need to avoid. The criterion for furthering the relationship then becomes: "Is this person capable of creating with me a relationship that is healthy, caring, and loving?"

The following section offers some tips for recognizing someone who might be abusive. These can help you make an informed decision and interrupt your "moth to the flame" pattern.

Warning Signals of an Abusive Partner

Laura, whom you met earlier in this chapter, entered her abusive relationship based on the man's charm and her intense attraction to him. Over time, she had difficulty recognizing both who he became (an abuser) and who she was (a confident woman).

When you're dating, attraction can distract you from initial warning signals. Preparing a written list of desirable and/or undesirable qualities ahead of time can make it easier to recognize those attributes in the moment. However, abusive people usually show you in the beginning the side you want to see and then change as you become more attached. They often start out treating you well—you may think you found your soul mate. It may not be until a few years later or after marriage that the relationship shifts and an abuser starts abusing. A list of cons, red flags, and deal-breakers can help

you evaluate if a love interest is or has stayed good. The following red flags can help predict trouble in the future:
- He/she does not accept your limits/boundaries or when you say no.
- He/she does not like your friends and does not want you to spend time with them.
- He/she slowly isolates you by finding flaws in your friends and family.
- He/she is very jealous.
- He/she is controlling and checks where you are all the time.
- He/she tells you how you should feel.
- He/she discounts your experience; for example, by claiming, "You're too sensitive."
- He/she is charming with others but becomes easily irritated with you when the two of you are alone.
- He/she makes you feel inferior in order to have more power and control over you.

***

This short list is inspired by a book by Patricia Evans (2003), called *Controlling People: How to Recognize, Understand and Deal with People Who Try to Control You.* The book lists many more red flags to watch for. If you feel that your partner leaves you disempowered, this is likely a sign that you are not in a healthy relationship. I encourage you to keep checking the list as you continue the relationship to make sure you are in the relationship you want and deserve.

Revising Your Childhood Love Script

In addition to memories of trauma, a child may carry into adulthood early bonding patterns and former family roles. Just because a child is now an adult doesn't mean these patterns will suddenly stop or that hurt feelings will be magically resolved. Being aware of your patterns won't, on its own, stop them either. The child is still within us, subconsciously acting out on a regular basis because it still wants to be heard, seen, loved, and properly addressed.

Sometimes you may find yourself feeling very young or regressed and even talk with a younger voice. There's a good chance that at the root of your destructive behaviors is a younger self.

By connecting and bonding to that part of you, you can eventually change your attachment style and unconscious family roles, allowing your adult self to act without the interference of the inner child. You can rescript your patterns—it is literally possible to create new neural pathways in the brain. Contacting your inner child for the first time may feel strange, because you simultaneously access two roles: the caregiver and the child. So how do you do it? My client Anna's story nicely illustrates this process.

Anna described having a deep sense of loneliness and depression. She showed signs of an avoidant attachment style in relationships, for example, picking men that were unavailable; she was also unwilling to be vulnerable and talk about feelings that could deepen her connection with men. Anna preferred meeting her partner once a week and was more comfortable watching TV together than talking. Ideally, they would be in the house together but not interact much. Sleeping close to someone felt stifling.

As she was searching for the answers to where these feelings originated, Anna used a visualization technique to contact her inner child. She received an image of herself when she was nine years old: Little Anna was feeling lonely, bored, and sad, waiting in her room for her mother to arrive home from work. However, Anna's mother was wrapped up in her own worries and fatigue and had become blind to her daughter's needs. Having lost the ability to be in tune with her daughter's emotional needs, her mother had become unavailable and emotionally distant—forms of neglect. Her mother's love wasn't consistent enough and Anna developed an avoidant attachment style.

During Anna's visualization, she came to a few realizations about herself, her parents, the world around her, and how she viewed love when she was young. She realized that as a child she had thought it was a burden for her mother to have to love her, and had felt that she needed to please her mother as much as she could in order to get attention and love in return. In general, she'd learned to rely on herself because her mother wasn't available. Anna would stay busy to distract herself from the pain of loneliness. A pattern of avoidant attachment, staying busy, seeking out unavailable people, and having to please everyone became ingrained in her. She eventually forgot where these habits had come from.

Adult Anna decided to communicate with her inner child and show her love on a regular basis. Building a deeper connection with her inner child took time and trust, but after a while, they formed a beautiful relationship. Adult Anna played with little Anna, made time for her, told her that she loved her, told her what was special about her, praised her, noticed and listened to her. Finally, little Anna was able to feel that it wasn't a burden for someone to love her, that love didn't require her to be self-reliant. Although Anna's childhood obviously couldn't change, her current habits and perceptions altered because she recognized that many were simply coping techniques that had been formed in the past and had no function anymore. As her relationship with herself improved, so did her feelings of loneliness and her relationships with others.

You, too, can find out what your inner child needs to hear. You, too, can communicate with your inner child. You may even be able to rewrite your script and tell your inner child how it should have been. The following exercise can help you start the process of connecting with the younger part within you.

Consoling Your Inner Child

1. Observe or ask your inner child or younger self what she/he needs.
2. Try to visualize and imagine that you fulfill your inner child's needs. You cannot provide different parents or circumstances, but you can take on the role of the parent and, for example, listen and see if your inner child needs attention. Maybe there wasn't enough loving attention growing up.

3. Now, to show your inner child that you care, inquire if she/he might like you to play with her/him.
4. Let your inner child guide you. If you were the parent of your inner child, what would you do? It's okay if you are still learning. This may be your first time acting as a parent. If you do not know how to act, go to a playground and observe other parents' interactions with their actual children, read books on how to be with a child, or discreetly ask a parent you know what they say to their children. Or just let your inner child teach you!
5. Most importantly, tell your younger self that you love and are there for her/him. Be honest. If you don't know how to interact or be present, tell your inner child that you are trying to learn and will look for help on how to be a parent.

***

For additional guidance through this process, you can check out books by

John Bradshaw, Erika J. Chopich and Margaret Paul, and Charles Whitfield, among others.

Why Your Heart Might Be Guarded after Trauma

Your traumatic experience may have led you to be extremely averse to being vulnerable, to avoid grief and other emotional pain, and to not trust what the future may bring. As you've tried to control your feelings, your heart may have become guarded or closed. If you want to unlock your heart—to feel more connection and mutual love—understanding why you've used this coping mechanism can help you move toward your goal. You may wish to try the exercise at the end of this chapter to slowly open your heart.

Loss of Control

Before your traumatic experience, you trusted that you and your family were safe in the world. Now you've lost that trust and feel you have no power or control over what happens to you.

Fear and love are both strong experiences that can make us feel vulnerable and powerless. As a result, they can seem especially risky to experience. Many traumatized people prefer that these feelings be avoided, controlled, or shielded. You might, for example, try to make your life more predictable by controlling your environment and feelings or those of others. When you try to control your feelings, however, you prevent your heart from being vulnerable, but also from being completely open.

After Maggie's husband died in a car accident, she didn't want to love again for fear her loved one would be taken away. Instead, she tried to control her feelings of romantic attraction and avoided the possibility of letting someone special into her life. Cindy, a mother whose son died during football practice, was so afraid of losing her second son that she tried to control his life. She observed that she felt most relaxed when everyone in the family was at home—because then she didn't have to worry about anyone dying. Cindy's relationship with her remaining son became strained, filled with frustrations and resentments; her son no longer wanted to come home anymore because she was so controlling. Although Cindy felt love for her second son, her fear and his anger put a cloud over their hearts.

There are many ways to attempt to assert control over yourself or others. Rarely, however, does either effort provide the assurance and true relief that one seeks—that is, to feel completely safe and/or to prevent a trauma from happening again. Instead, constant attempts to gain—or give up—control can foster frustration and resentment in loved ones, prompting internal walls and withdrawal.

Away from Pain

Another way you may have tried to shield your heart from vulnerability is to disconnect, avoid, or distance yourself from painful feelings such as grief. This is especially so when past grief is unresolved. Trauma such as war, sudden death, or natural disaster often brings heavy losses.

Working through the five stages of grieving (Kübler-Ross and Kessler 2007), consciously and patiently, is an important part of healing from such terrible experiences. In the process, you encounter painful emotions such as denial, anger, and guilt, accompanied with constant or intermittent sadness. It's normal to be in denial at first, to not fully believe that this happened to you. Next can come anger, possibly expressed by blaming others for various things. The third stage—one that has been very hard for many of my clients to overcome—is bargaining and guilt. This includes thoughts like, "If I only hadn't done this or that, then [the traumatic event] wouldn't have happened." The fourth stage involves deep sadness and depression, often with uncontrollable crying and a loss of interest in everything, including food. When grieving individuals have passed through all of these emotions and experiences, they usually arrive at the final phase: acceptance. Everyone, however, has a unique way of grieving and recovering. You may go back and forth among the stages or take longer in some than the others. Avoiding any of these feelings may cause you to get stuck in the cycle and become depressed, anxious, irritated, and isolated.

When we become stuck reacting to or avoiding certain emotions, one or more emotions may become poorly developed or over-or underused. I have many clients who can never show anger, only sadness. Others feel irritation, impatience, and anger all the time but have difficulty accessing sorrow. Some people stay in a state of fear or numbness and have a hard time feeling any other emotion and consequently remain in their head most of the time, trying to be analytical. Often, whatever emotion was most necessary for self-preservation during the traumatic event will become overdeveloped. The feeling that was repressed or unavailable will become the weakest. The psyche and body then have to compensate for these feelings. Please know that you had to cope somehow—there's no reason to feel bad about this. However, now that the trauma is over, you need to make sure you can access all your emotions equally again. Start by determining what is your "go to" emotion, and which emotions have disappeared from your vocabulary or aren't easy to access but need to be found again.

When I was younger, my self-preservation relied on my not getting angry. For a long period of my life, I was unable to be angry. While anger can range in intensity from irritation to frustration to rage, I associated anger with overpowering another person with physical violence or hurting someone with verbal attacks. As a result, I saw anger as destructive and shut down the feeling. I was, further, frightened of anyone who expressed anger. Because I wouldn't let myself feel anger, my body had to compensate somehow. Holding in my feelings led to physical constrictions, stomachaches, and ulcers, and also caused me to hold onto resentment. Anger, as I found out, can be a helpful emotion; it's not anger that's damaging, it's how you use it.

In fact, when used properly, anger can be a very important feeling, because it warns us that something is wrong. Anger can motivate us to take action about a situation and provide us with extra emotional—and even physical—strength when we need it. Anger, however, is complicated. There are people who aren't in touch with their anger and don't know they are angry. There are those who feel anger but don't know how to express it. There are those who feel overwhelmed by their anger, and others who use anger inappropriately.

As with fear, anxiety, and depression, anger is a common reaction to trauma. Some people try to mask fear or depression with anger. For me, because anger wasn't in my vocabulary, my sadness had to protect my anger. A former therapist once told me that it would take at least three years to access and overcome my suppressed anger. I stopped going to him because that seemed too long and made me feel hopeless. In the end, it probably took almost that long with another therapist, but my hope that it would take less time helped me get through the process. Meanwhile, because I was detached from my anger, my sadness became overdeveloped.

Sometimes my sadness would become so strong that the only way I could deal with it was to sleep for hours or an entire day, which led to further isolation. There were many days and weekends spent that way. Not being able to be angry also kept me from expressing myself and brought distance to my social interactions because I had a hard time letting go of resentments and annoyances. Fortunately, now I can usually access and express my anger appropriately and no longer find it debilitating and unpleasant. While being angry can still feel uncomfortable, lack of access to my anger no longer deters me from connecting to others or myself.

Reconnecting with Emotions

It is important to reconnect to dormant, repressed, or disconnected emotions. The more connected you are to yourself, the more you can open your heart, connect to others, and build emotional intimacy and support. Try not to discriminate against any type of feeling—doing so only disconnects you from yourself and others. When people are able to feel their real feelings, when they grieve fully and heal their trauma, they can often go beyond habitual defenses. In my own personal work, I learned that, *as you discover yourself, you discover who others truly are.* We often project our fears and feelings onto others; without those fears we are able to perceive others as who they really are.

As the authors of *Undefended Love* note, intimacy is a feeling of a deep connection not only with others but also within us (Psaris and Lyons 2000). When you achieve that relationship within yourself, you feel at peace. When you connect to yourself, you become better able to be in the moment; you move away from being stuck in the past or the future. You take care of your needs and are able to share yourself with an *appropriate* person. You know that you are worthy of joy and happiness (Mills and Turnbull 2004).

The ability to love yourself and others develops from being in touch with your emotions and sensations and feeling safe with them. To connect with ourselves and others, we must first access repressed feelings and learn to not only tolerate but lovingly manage them. When we are able to be vulnerable and trust our feelings, we are ready to open our heart. When our heart is open we can give and receive love. As Brené Brown, an author and research professor, said in a TED talk: "Vulnerability is the birthplace of joy and happiness" (2010).

The next exercise offers you steps for accessing and tolerating your emotions; it can be done alone or with a therapist or supportive friend. These steps don't involve revisiting traumatic events or your past. They do, however, help you begin the process of feeling familiar and safe with your own emotions and bodily reactions. Please, take small steps so that the gate to your emotions doesn't open too rapidly and overwhelm you with feelings. If you start to feel anxious, overwhelmed, or scared during the exercises, slow down and take a deep slow breath. If this exercise brings up too much, practice the self-soothing techniques you learned in chapter 2 and/or connect with your therapist or support group while you slowly explore dormant emotions.

Your emotions need to be not just named, but located and sensed in the body, listened to, and expressed. Pay attention to and follow the sensations that correlate with your emotion. You can practice this exercise with any emotion, such as anxiety, fear, sadness, and so on—simply replace the word "anger" with the emotion of your choice.

Ten Powerful Steps to Unlock Your Heart

1. Choose a comfortable place where you won't be interrupted. Look around until you find something soothing to view. This might be a plant, a picture, a candle, a tree outside a window, or something else. Once you find a soothing object, hang out for a few minutes until you feel calm or at least calmer.
2. Name your negative emotion; for example, say, "I am angry." Articulating your emotions as

words both acknowledges and expresses them; it also has a positive effect on your amygdala, which is in communication with your nervous system and fight-flight-freeze reaction.

3. Locate your emotion. For example, when I did this exercise, I became aware of constriction in my throat, butterflies in my stomach, and a slight headache.
4. Sense your emotion. The physical sensations connected to your emotions can serve as your warning signals—they can help you recognize that you need to pay attention to your emotion and can minimize delayed reactions. I learned that whenever I was experiencing these physical sensations, I needed to explicitly check in with myself about what had just happened and if I was angry. Because I had delayed emotional responses, I wasn't always aware of my anger in the moment otherwise.
5. Focus on the sensation in your body. Is it tolerable? If so, allow

yourself to have the emotion and related sensations without trying to escape them. If it remains tolerable, you can continue. If not, choose a scenario that is less charged or reach out to a somatic therapist. The beauty is that, once you pay attention to them, most often these intense feelings will shift.

6. While staying connected to your sensations, express your emotions through gesture, posture, movement, drawing, song, or anything else. For example, I made a fist while saying, "I am angry." Pay attention to your sensations as you express your emotions this way.

7. Give whatever form of expression you have chosen—gesture, movement, posture, and so on—time to unfold until you feel it is completed. For example, your fist might want to open, your chest might want to bend over and then open up. You may be surprised by what your body does. As long as it is safe, try to follow

your body. You may even come up with a new song, dance, picture, or similar.
8. End by finding something soothing in your environment again. Whatever it may be, focus on it for a few minutes until you feel calmer. Observe how your body knows how to calm down.
9. List any new insights you're taking away from this experience.
10. Be compassionate with yourself and praise yourself for working on your tough issues.

***

You can practice this exercise with any emotion. Check in with yourself periodically to see if anger—or any other emotion—is brewing unnoticed. A daily log can be helpful to see what situations trigger your emotions, how you respond, and to check if there are other responses available. For me, connecting to my anger brought me closer to myself. Expressing it appropriately to others brought me closer to them because I stopped harboring resentments.

Make a list of what helps you when emotions surface. For example, when I'm angry, I try to communicate directly what I am angry about. If I'm angry at a person I can't express my feelings to, I talk it through with a friend or therapist or write in a journal. If your anger at another person becomes too strong, you may need to take some time to yourself and walk around the block before expressing it. Let the other person know that you're going to cool off and will return when you feel calmer. Some people express their feelings by drawing, dancing, or doing other kinds of art. What's on your list?

Conclusion: Healing the Trauma Blueprint

You may have been told that you have to love yourself before anyone can love you, but loving yourself can be extremely hard when your feelings are disconnected due to trauma, you never felt loved as a child, or your bond was severed due to abuse, loss, or separation from your parent. As David Schnarch, author and renowned sex and marital therapist, notes, "taking care of your own feelings is an integral part of maintaining a relationship and how it fuels attachment" (Schnarch 1997, 43). When you feel connected to yourself, you can start connecting with others. When people mutually connect, you can experience love. Connection allows you to gain—or regain—emotional intimacy. This, in turn, can lead to love: loving yourself and feeling loved by others.

Even if you don't have or desire a romantic partner in your life, it's vital to address any emotional disconnects you may have, especially those related to trauma. Steadily working to access your emotions and practicing how to use them appropriately will bring you closer to yourself and enhance your ability to relate to others in all aspects of your life. Be honest with yourself: Would you truly prefer locking out certain feelings? Consider the emotional and physical consequences of that—and what you could gain by having the use of that feeling again. As you gently probe your thoughts, you'll likely realize that this feeling is an integral part of human emotional makeup and self-expression. Know that the effort to incorporate it once again can be extremely rewarding. If you are having interpersonal difficulties and/or inner conflict such as anxiety or depression, or feel as if you have never known love in your entire life, ask yourself, "What have I got to lose by trying?" Life *can* be better! If you weren't treated with kindness and love growing up, you may feel unworthy of receiving love now. Let me assure you: you are lovable and deserve to be loved.

CHAPTER 4

Sexual Healing

"A caress should say 'I love you,' not pay off a debt. An embrace should fill the heart as well as the arms."
—Hugh and Gail Prather

This chapter delves into the sexual troubles trauma may have caused you, and why you may experience difficulties with touch of any kind, sensual or non-sensual, even just a hug. It also provides advice and exercises that will help you relax and feel safe enough to sense pleasure and be aroused sexually again. It's not only sexual abuse survivors who struggle with opening up to and enjoying sex. *Know that it's not the type of trauma experienced that can cause sexual difficulties or dysfunction, but the long-term effects of trauma.* If the root of the problem is your trauma, then that is what needs attention and to be healed. If you experience sexual problems for other reasons, you'll want to investigate if these are primarily caused by a medical, personal, relationship, or trauma issue.

What Is a Normal Sex Life?

It's helpful to establish what your normal sex life is so that you can recognize when there's a problem and prevent worry when there isn't one. Many couples worry there is something wrong with them if they aren't sexually active a certain number of times a week or month. There's a common belief that couples have to meet a particular sexual requirement or status quo in order to keep a healthy relationship. This is not true: A small amount or lack of sexual interaction doesn't necessarily mean a couple isn't in love with each other or lacks mutual attraction, or that there is a problem. In fact, good relationships can have many different patterns of sexual interaction, including couples who are sexually intimate once or multiple times a day, once a week, and once a month, as well as numerous couples who rarely or even never have physical intimacy.

As Heather Howard, a sex educator in San Francisco, explains, the education we receive about sex focuses predominantly on reproductive function—as a result, many people consider only intercourse "normal," which yields a focus on men's orgasms over women's orgasms. However, intercourse "is not the optimal method for orgasm in many females, as the homologous organ to the sensitive penile glans is the clitoral glans, which is located above rather than inside the vagina" (personal communication 2017).

Many women don't experience orgasms during intercourse and wonder if that's normal. Statistics vary, but generally show that most women (up to 85 percent) don't orgasm during intercourse, and some (about 5 percent) don't experience orgasms during any sexual activity; concerns about disappointing their partners, however, cause many women to fake orgasms (Lloyd 2006).

So, what is normal sex? There is no norm—healthy sex varies widely in terms of sexual desire, frequency, and styles, and can depend on age, health, lifestyle, parenthood, fatigue, length of relationship, and libido. As long as *all* individuals agree on all fronts of their intimacy, there is no problem. Sexual problems are bound to arise in relationships and sometimes they will surface to bring to light current personal and/or relationship issues. When addressed properly, such situations can be opportunities for growth (Schnarch 1997). More serious problems emerge, however, when intimacy problems such as erectile dysfunction, experiencing pain during intercourse, and being averse to touch are due to suffering from PTSD, depression, and anxiety. Now, your body and your psyche are warning you that something isn't right and urging you to listen and do something about it. No matter what the root cause, issues in the bedroom can make a relationship vulnerable to resentment, frustration, and feelings of rejection or being undesirable.

Erotic Pleasure and Desire after Trauma

Many individuals wonder if they are in the right relationship when they don't experience sexual desire or face sexual difficulties with their partner. Sexual issues may or may not be fully related to a current relationship—they may be the outcome of traumatic experiences. One study found that roughly 90 percent of women with PTSD report sexual dysfunction (Yehuda, Lehrer, and Rosenbaum 2015). Similarly, research has found that veterans show an elevated risk of sexual problems due to PTSD (Solomon 1993). Survivors of other types of trauma can show similar intimacy issues (Mills 2001, in Mills and Turnbull 2004), including people who have experienced car accidents (DeSilva 1999).

Why? This is because after an accident, birth trauma, loss of a loved one, near-death experience, natural disaster, abuse, or any other trauma, the sympathetic nervous system is on alert and wants to protect the body

(Bremner et al. 1996). Sexual arousal can elevate this alert mode and may trigger trauma associations as a result (Rellini and Meston 2006). Involuntary reactions to such trauma associations may in turn connect the sensations of arousal to feeling fearful, threatened, or hyperaware, and thus impede healthy sexual function and closeness. Additionally, flashbacks, memories, and intense emotions can cause constriction and tension in the body, or cause the body to shut down (Goulston 2008). Such shutting down is a form of dissociation; it's often experienced as feeling frozen and unable to move or feel. Reactions can occur not only during sex but during any sexual arousal, including attraction for someone you see or arousal from watching sexual movies.

Both sexual and nonsexual trauma can lead to a number of difficulties with physical intimacy, including fear, avoidance, or numbing of sexual arousal; constriction and physical discomfort during sex; erectile dysfunction, inability to orgasm, low or no sex drive, or sex addiction. In addition, many people with PTSD take medications that can have physical or emotional side effects that contribute to intimacy struggles.

For some people, because they've had PTSD symptoms from a young age, they've never developed a sex drive and have nothing to compare against their current experience. Others try to deal with sexual difficulties in a variety of ways, with some becoming involved with paradoxical sexual behaviors, "such as trying to obtain closeness from a distance, e.g., pornography, commercial sex phone lines, etc." (Mills and Turnbull 2004, 274).

Like many, trauma survivors want to enjoy intimacy and a healthy sex life but don't know how to achieve these goals, or are too ashamed to do something about their problems. If you feel like this or have a partner who feels like this, you are not alone. Most likely these problems can be resolved. Unfortunately, topics related to sexual issues and trauma are seldom talked about, but if we know *why* and *when* we react a certain way, we can figure out *how* to address a problem. Intimacy issues can have various causes; here we explore when trauma is the root of problems, in particular when the body is shutting down sexually.

Shutting Down Sexually

Any trauma can lead to shutting down sexually. Such shutting down can show up in a variety of ways, including discomfort with touch of any kind, experiencing sex as painful (for example, suffering from vaginismus or tense vaginal muscles), and lack of interest in sex.

"Don't Touch Me"

As humans, our first bonding experience and feeling of connection starts in infancy. Research shows that touch helps develop infants' brains and facilitates infants' bonds with their parents and caregivers. When infants don't get enough appropriate touch, they can develop lifelong emotional disturbances or even die (Ardiel and Rankin 2010). Touch isn't only imperative to the emotional wellbeing and survival of infants—adults benefit from it as well. This is due to the release of oxytocin, a hormone with relaxing, calming, and bonding qualities. Therefore, difficulties with touch can interfere with bonding and establishing closeness.

It's important to know what you're comfortable with in a relationship, in regard to both sexual and nonsexual touch. For one person, touch such as hugs and massages can feel wonderful; another person may experience the same touch as unpleasant or repulsive due to associations with trauma (Goulston 2008). I've had people describe this to me as having a "skin memory," with touch in some places yielding pleasure, in others anger. My client Leonie had trouble whenever anyone touched her hair, because it triggered memories of her father pulling her hair violently.

"Intercourse Is Too Painful": Vaginismus

Tara was dating a wonderful man she felt comfortable with. Intercourse, though, wasn't possible. They tried long foreplay, additional lubrication, and not taking sex too seriously. She went to a gynecologist to rule out physical problems and learned there was nothing wrong with her physically or hormonally. Tara decided to look at it from a different angle and brought it up in therapy. The problem, she explained, wasn't a lack of desire for sex, but rather, she thought, that Bert (her boyfriend) was too well endowed. Every time they tried to have intercourse, they ended up having to stop. Tara experienced pain and muscle spasms, and Bert would lose his erection. She reported that they were confused and frustrated. They didn't know if the sizes of their genitals were physically incompatible—that is, if they just didn't fit together—or if the problem was that Bert couldn't sustain his erection.

During therapy, Tara realized that her body was reacting to their intimacy. She was suffering from "vaginismus," a kind of muscle tightness that can cause pain during intercourse, gynecological exams, or when inserting a tampon. (In addition to trauma, vaginismus can be caused by associations with past painful experiences, relationship problems, fear of becoming pregnant, tensing up from nervousness, or never having had successful sexual experiences before (Silverstein 1989).) Although Tara trusted, felt attracted to, and had the desire to be sexual with Bert, every time they tried to be intimate, she tensed up. She discovered that her inability to relax during intercourse—along with her inhibited sexual identity—stemmed from traumatic experiences in her childhood.

Bedroom issues can feel overwhelming and go to the core of your or your partner's self-esteem. Bert could have taken Tara's issue the wrong way and thought she wasn't attracted enough to him, or that she didn't like him enough, as many partners start to believe. Fortunately, Tara and Bert worked hard to communicate from the start about their problems having intercourse and were able to negotiate alternative solutions.

Tara was surprised to learn that even though she hadn't been sexually abused, her traumatic childhood experiences could have impacted her physical intimacy. I explained that part of being sexual is letting go of control. Letting go of control can be hard for anyone who has experienced trauma, because it evokes feelings of powerlessness and vulnerability. She felt that was true for her.

With this in mind, Tara reexamined her childhood. She grew up with a psychologically abusive mother who suffered from severe paranoia personality disorder and consequently was unusually suspicious of everyone and controlling. (Please note, there are many variations of mental disorders, and people with the same disorder can be more or less functional—it is not by any means a given that mental illness leads to abuse.) Her mother instilled deep fear in her, constantly warning her of unrealistic danger.

As is true with many abused children, Tara never felt safe and wasn't allowed to express herself as a person. Additionally, she always tried to lessen her mom's fears by doing only what her mother felt didn't risk harm. She wished that she could have dressed more feminine growing up, "but there was so much paranoia about it from my mother that I shut down my femininity ... I became stiff, rigid, and serious." Tara didn't have the opportunity to develop her own identity because that would have seemed too much of a threat to her mom.

Tara realized that, as a result, she was still in constant survival mode and always trying to control her feelings. Tara decided to work on finding her identity, being vulnerable but powerful, and letting go of control. Changing beliefs, finding or regaining individuality, resolving negative associations, and overcoming fight-flight-freeze reactions don't occur overnight. And such difficulties can be complicated by other factors: the body can tense up for many different reasons, and sexual problems can make one feel like a failure and a partner feel unloved. Still, over a few weeks of therapy, Tara noticed that she was getting more relaxed. As time passed, she was eventually able to relax sufficiently to enjoy sexual intercourse with Bert.

"Sex Doesn't Interest Me": Posttraumatic Relationship

Laura, who was mentioned earlier, had a wonderful sex life, with intense chemistry, at the beginning of her relationship. Then a shift occurred: her body shut down and she could no longer enjoy physical intimacy. Laura's body and psyche were trying to tell her something about her current relationship—and possibly her unresolved past—that she wasn't aware of. Laura was confused. Her strong sexual connection with her husband had made her believe that he was "the one." The intensity of her attraction to him was so deep that she couldn't imagine having such chemistry with anyone else. "We had a very strong sexual relationship," Laura explained to me, "the strongest of my life. We had a lot of sex every week, and I mean like, you know, maybe four times, or five times a week, sometimes every day."

While a special attraction for someone you care about can be a wonderful feeling, it may not mean the two of you are compatible, and can obscure your perception of who the person really is. Attraction can be a signal of various things going on. The other person may not be the full reason for what you think and feel. Other possibilities include: 1) your attraction may be due to the fact that the person feels familiar, evoking something in your past; 2) the magnetism you feel may come from your nervous system looking for an adrenaline rush so that you stay in fight-or-flight preparation mode; or 3) a strong desire for someone may also indicate something about your beliefs or attachment style, or reflect parts in you that need growth. Of course, attraction can indicate a wonderful connection as well, but be careful: *Attraction just tells you that your hormones are activated. It doesn't tell you anything about the person—without more information, you can't know if you are with the right person.*

Laura didn't know why her body had started to shut down and her desire to be intimate had faded. She told me, "It was always very good, but suddenly I found that I didn't want to have sex anymore and I couldn't open up to him. I'd shut down." Shutting down or dissociation is a way to remove yourself emotionally and physically. It's different from a lack of desire. Dissociation is a stronger feeling in which you withdraw and feel disconnected.

Laura wanted to know how to stop shutting down. As a coping strategy, dissociation is not uncommon for people in—or recovering from—abusive relationships, as well as for those suffering from trauma not caused by a partner. I explored both possibilities with Laura. Questions about Laura's husband revealed that he was degrading and minimizing her. He got angry easily and then blamed her for his reaction. He was also very controlling. As we talked more about her husband, she realized that his behavior was a form of emotional abuse.

Laura began to understand that her body was alerting her that there was something wrong in her relationship. Her body and psyche were using shutting down as a coping mechanism to guard her vulnerability and defend against the possibility of being harmed. These reactions had been learned over time as she was exposed to her husband's abuse. Laura realized that the intense sexual energy at the beginning of the relationship had clouded her perspective. Having good chemistry or regular sex is not always a sign of a good relationship, nor does it indicate that a partner is the right one.

Laura left her abusive husband and eventually entered another relationship. This new relationship was emotionally healthy, but her sex life wasn't as regular or as intense as she had experienced with her ex-husband. Over time, her body had learned that it didn't have to shut down anymore. Her new partner's desire for sex, however, was less than hers.

This time around, deep conversations led to deep intimacy. As she explained, "When this relationship started out, sex wasn't the dominating factor. It was the relationship, or the coming together of two people—the discussions and the talking—that was the dominating factor. Sex took a backseat." This new relationship focused on communication, interaction, and compatibility. Sex was just something that accompanied those, and she was content with that. As she pointed out, she'd already had a relationship that was incredibly sexual and it was the most destructive one of her life. She smiled, "And, you know, if I have to supplement my sexuality a little on the side by myself privately, then I will do that, but I'm in the happiest relationship that I've ever been in. And I would never sacrifice that because I want to make love a couple more times a week."

Michelle, another client, explained that a strong sexual chemistry was the main reason why she began dating her boyfriend. Even after he tried to kill her and she had taken out a restraining order against him, the sexual chemistry was so strong that she pursued the relationship once more. Michelle was afraid she would never again experience this type of "electricity." Unlike Laura, Michelle's body didn't shut down sexually. It did, however, signal to her that something was wrong: Michelle began experiencing high levels of anxiety. It was this anxiety that initially brought Michelle to my office. Michelle, like so many people, asked, "Why am I so attracted to someone like him [or her]?" In therapy, she came to ask, "Why am I staying when it is obviously the wrong person?"

> "Why am I staying when it is obviously the wrong person?"
>
> One possible answer to this question is that we can mistake intense attraction for a sign of compatibility or love—even when our logical mind is telling us that the relationship isn't good for us or is downright dysfunctional. That pull feels like a magnet we can't resist; we feel we cannot live without the other person.
>
> Another point to consider is that a "trauma bond"—that is, a bond between an abuser and a victim—creates a particular type of intensity by using extreme opposites intermittently. These might be, for example, caring and fear, closeness and abandonment, making one laugh

and then cry, talking and silent treatment, tenderness and violence, and so on. This creates a "time arousal-jag"—that is, a hormonal response that occurs when an increase in arousal (such as from fear) is followed by abrupt low arousal (from caring), making it harder for the victims to leave. This is often a major factor in an abusive relationship.

A perpetrator usually uses charm, trust, and/or authority to win a victim over—and then exploits and manipulates the victim later. This can happen in domestic relationships, as well as between a boss and employee, doctor and patient, priest and congregation member, yoga teacher and student, or any relationship where there is a power differential. Victims of trauma bonding can be of any age, gender, race, or socioeconomic status.

Initially, to gain power and control, the perpetrator may try to fulfill the victim's deepest emotional desires, such as to be loved, taken care of, or accepted. The perpetrator may then switch to isolation techniques, so that the victim has no resources to leave and becomes dependent. The perpetrator will also criticize, degrade, manipulate, dehumanize, and make the victim feel helpless and insecure, so that the victim is flooded with self-doubt and feels both that the abuse is somehow deserved and that leaving isn't possible. Victims are left feeling crazy.

Such abusers are highly skilled in finding victims and making/keeping them dependent. Victims may not be conscious of these tactics. In hindsight, you may recognize that the relationship was unhealthy, abusive, or not the right one. Your vulnerabilities and needs likely weren't as clear at that time as they are now. To one degree or another, most of us can be and have been manipulated, coaxed, or innocently drawn into relationships that seemed to have great potential. Please be assured: it was not your fault.

Orienting Toward Relaxation

If you're in a nontoxic relationship but still experience difficulty with enjoying touch, you first need to learn how to relax your body. Then, explore how to sense pleasure by yourself. After that, you can work up to enjoying sexual pleasure from your partner. The following two exercises will help you begin this process.

It can be difficult to feel pleasure when your body is tense and constricted. Therefore, it's important to teach your body that it is safe to relax and feel intensity. I recommend practicing the Jacobson progressive muscle relaxation technique developed by Edmund Jacobson (1946). This technique concentrates on tightening and relaxing muscle groups—without inflicting pain—in a particular order. This can relax the body and mind and lead to a lessening of anxiety. When applied in the context of trauma recovery, it can be used to minimize anxiety about sex, touch, closeness, or any other anxiety. You can find details about

Jacobson's technique in many books and articles, as well as on YouTube.

How to Relax Your Body

As you move through this exercise, tightening and relaxing your muscles, each time, notice the sensations associated with these changes. Observe, too, what you feel before and after the exercise.

1. Curl your toes under. Hold the tension for a moment. Relax your toes. One leg at a time, move up your calf muscles, tightening and relaxing.
2. Move on to squeezing your buttocks and then abdomen muscles. Release them.
3. Raise your shoulders and tighten your neck. Drop your shoulders.
4. Make a fist with your hands. Open the fist.
5. Open your mouth wide. Close it. Let your tongue relax.
6. Raise your forehead. Lower it.

Do this exercise once a day for one week—or as often as you feel necessary—before you start exploring non-erotic self-touch. Note: after practicing this relaxation technique, please make sure you are sufficiently alert before beginning another activity.

***

Notice if anything comes up for you when you tense or relax your muscles. Some people aren't comfortable with the feelings and sensations of relaxation. Others experience anxiety and other unpleasant emotions and sensations when tensing their muscles. As you pay attention to your body, notice, too, that even after you think you've let go of all tension, you can probably relax even more deeply.

This exercise isn't just for people who want to learn to experience erotic pleasure, it's a general relaxation technique. It's essential to learn to relax. Being able to change your level of muscle and nervous tension is vital to making other changes necessary to heal and increase your feelings of ease and functionality.

How to Feel Safe to Sense Pleasure

Please know that you deserve to enjoy sensual pleasure and desire. You are worthy of healing. You are worthy of enjoying touch—both nonsexual and sexual—and erotic pleasure. Can you give yourself permission to enjoy erotic pleasure now or in the future? Reframe the following sentence with anything that brings positive associations: "I allow myself to _____ and _____." Pause, and let that settle in for a moment. What do you notice in your body?

Begin your exploration of self-touch before you explore being touched by a lover or a loved one. Heather Howard, PhD, a sexologist who helps individuals meet their sexual and intimate goals, recommends touching your own body with your fingers, a feather, or even gently with water. She suggests starting with body parts that you personally consider less sensitive and not overtly sexual. For some people, this might be hands, arms, scalp, and feet; others, however, might consider those areas sexual (Howard, personal communication 2017). This is one way to begin to familiarize yourself with your feelings—especially the ones you find you have been out of contact with for one reason or another.

Notice what feels good and gives you pleasure. Vary the stimulation to learn what you like. Practice touch for only as long as you can remain present and focused on the sensation. Over time, try to extend how long you can remain present. After you've familiarized yourself with your body in a nonsexual way, slowly and gradually—over days, weeks, months, or however long it takes—learn to be sensual and sexual with your own body. Expand your touch to increasingly sensitive and sexual areas of your body, eventually including your genitals. As you build your ability to remain present with sensation and intensity, consider allowing yourself to become sexually aroused, to build your nervous system's ability to safely sustain arousal.

It's important to focus on your touch and your sensations without judging yourself. You have a beautiful body with amazing biological abilities—learn to understand that. Explore what feels good to you. This shows your body that you respect it. Your body deserves to be respected, not critiqued or shunned. Be patient with yourself and do not put yourself under pressure. Don't let your mind wander. Notice what feels good and what gives you erotic pleasure. This exercise is intended to make new associations, to help you relax and feel safe when you experience sexual feelings. Pay attention and gauge what creates arousal and what does not.

Explore slow, deep, rhythmic breathing. If your breath is shallow and high in your chest, begin to breathe all the way down into your stomach instead. When you breathe slowly, you are telling your nervous system that you are safe. See if you can relax your stomach and widen your abdomen as you breathe in. Now, try to relax your legs and pelvis. If you have trouble with this, try tensing them up and then releasing them, as in the previous exercise.

When you feel comfortable with your own touch and the erotic feelings that you induce, you can start to explore nonsexual and sexual touch with a partner. Sex therapist Barbara Keesling (2006) suggests that couples schedule a time to explore consensual touch together. Don't dismiss the time that is set aside for this—be mentally and physically prepared to explore together.

Just as in the self-touch exercise, the room should feel comfortable and have a relaxing atmosphere. There should be no expectation to perform, only an intention to explore healing. When you are both ready, move slowly from nonsexual touch to erotic touch. You'll know you are ready when you don't feel anxious and you enjoy the touch.

Start by having your partner caress your shoulders, hands, feet, or whatever areas you would like to start with. Rate each area and type of touch from 1 to 10 on how good it feels, 10 being the best. Many people expect their partner to read them fluently—to know when they aren't satisfied or when sex isn't working for them. These expectations can lead to disappointment and disconnection. Communication, on the other hand, can bring solutions and closeness. Learn and communicate about what touch feels good for you and your partner.

If at any point you become anxious, please don't suppress your emotions. Instead, listen to your body. What is your body telling you? Anxiety is your nervous system's way of alerting you that your survival mode may be activated. If this happens, try to find another touch that is less activating so that you can enter or remain in the relaxed mode of the parasympathetic nervous system. Anxiety can express itself as worry about performance, impatience, loss of arousal, and muscle tightness, among others. The more often you can associate erotic touch with relaxation, the less anxiety you will experience during arousal in the long run. If you don't find any touch relaxing, you may want to seek the help of a sex therapist—sex therapists have many, many ideas about how to help. Another option is to begin with Barbara Keesling's book *Sexual Healing: A*

Complete Guide To Overcoming Common Sexual Problems, which offers many exercises, as well as a chapter on severe sexual fears.

Conclusion: Addressing Physical Intimacy Problems

No matter what they are, physical intimacy problems can put healthy relationships to the test and create difficulties in entering new relationships. Sexual issues, including shutting down in response to sexual intimacy, are common among trauma survivors because the body is on alert to avoid anything that might prompt negative memories and associations. Know that when you understand and change your reactions to physical intimacy, you can create new patterns in both your mind and body.

There is help for sexual difficulties. It might seem that talking to a professional such as a sex therapist would be embarrassing. The worst fear and awkwardness, however, arises before the session. For most who finally make the appointment, talking to someone who is comfortable with the topic of sexuality normalizes the discussion, reducing embarrassment or shame. A professional can help you find the best solutions. (By the way, a sex therapist—or any other therapist—does *not* have sexual interactions with a client. That would be illegal!)

If you don't want to see a therapist in person or can't afford treatment, many books and online resources are available. Most important is your desire to patiently address your sexual blocks with positive intention, self-education, and experimentation. Such experimentation will include gentle forays into what is currently uncomfortable or unfamiliar territory for you. A certified sex surrogate can be a legitimate option.

> ### A Sex Surrogate Is a Legitimate Option
>
> Those who are inclined to explore independently, or who do not have a partner to help heal their sexual issues, can work with a certified surrogate partner. A surrogate partner

is much more than a substitute for a sex partner. A surrogate partner serves as a professional educator, helping people improve their capacity for emotional and physical intimacy and heal their sexual wounds through a series of structured exercises. Surrogate partners are paid for helping, healing, and educating someone, not for sex, though sexual contact may be a part of the program if clinically indicated. As Barbara Keesling describes, a first session typically involves discussing sexual issues and may continue with "sensate-focus touching exercises" (2006, 17).

CHAPTER 5

Creating a Trauma-Resilient Relationship

"The foundation of a relationship is being able to be vulnerable and unguarded."
—Jett Psaris and Marlena Lyons

As we discussed in the previous chapter, trauma effects can interfere with your romantic relationships. This is especially so for when suffering from PTSD, with its general feelings of being disconnected and not safe. At the same time, it's important to reconnect after a trauma; reconnecting can give you a sense of safety and support your recovery. Loving and compassionate communication about your needs and triggers, as well as sharing your grief and hurt, can help you accomplish this. That said, communication can be difficult, as trauma triggers can cause us to overreact.

This chapter provides important tools to help strengthen the foundation of your primary relationship and make it more trauma-resilient. The following pages explore how to be vulnerable when you want to guard yourself; how to boost the hormones that help you connect with your partner when you feel disconnected; how best to address conflict when you want to avoid it; how to sense your boundaries rather than set up walls; and how to receive support from your relationships, romantic and otherwise. All of these strategies can create resilience, helping you respond in healthy ways to stress within a relationship.

Dare to Be Vulnerable

Many trauma survivors have to make a concerted effort to learn to trust again. It takes courage to open up and expose those parts of yourself that you're afraid another won't like—or that you might not like yourself. You may fear being hurt again and may not feel safe opening up. Maybe you're afraid your vulnerability will be used against you. You may also worry about the questions you could be asked once you share, or may feel that you are a burden. Actually, *not* sharing can confuse partners and cause them to negatively misinterpret your behavior when they don't know why you're reacting a certain way. Your partner may take it personally when you suddenly shut down, feel emotional, or are triggered in other ways. When you open up, you don't have to give details about what happened to you—you can keep it simple, particularly in the beginning, and just say that you've experienced some trauma that causes you to have certain reactions. (Please word it however feels most comfortable to you.)

The benefits of sharing are many. Sharing can provide you with a sense of freedom—you no longer have to hold in or hide your story. Another benefit can be improved bonding as the walls that protect vulnerability come down. When we let our walls down with others, they may feel inclined to share as well, bringing you closer together.

For example, after a month of dating, Michael decided to tell the woman who would become his beloved third wife about his traumatic history and triggers. He trusted her enough to feel comfortable doing so. This gave his future spouse permission to share as well. "Immediately," he told me, "that was a bond that we shared ... We trusted each other with a secret that we wouldn't tell everybody." Of course, whom we share with is important. Unfortunately, many of us don't share even when we have a trustworthy person in our life. If you have a good person to share with, the following exercise can help you open up and share while staying balanced and connected to yourself.

Healthy Sharing

When talking about your trauma, pace yourself so that you don't get overwhelmed. Watch to see if your body is signaling to you that it's okay to continue with your story, or if you need to stop. If you feel sudden tension, such as a headache, you may need to pause. Watch, too, for clues that show you whether the other person is becoming overwhelmed. Your partner may have a "deer in headlights" look, or become intense, anxious, or confused.

Before you begin to talk about your trauma, slow down your breath and rate of speech. As you share, slow down your breath and speech again whenever you feel your emotions rising. This will slow your heart rate and keep emotions from getting ahead of you.

As you speak, look into your partner's eyes: know you are loved or cared for and not in danger. Is your partner asking too many questions? Explain that you'll need to answer questions one at a time, or that for now you won't answer questions so that you don't become overwhelmed.

While you share your story and your emotions, you may also want to tell your partner or friend what reaction you are looking for or fear, such as, "Please don't laugh," or, "Please don't pity me." Educate your companion: offer resources such as articles and books about trauma so that you can receive the support and understanding you need.

Give Your Love Relationship an Oxytocin Boost

Traumatic experiences, old or new, can uproot a relationship. Combinations of PTSD symptoms and increased levels of stress hormones such as cortisol can make you feel disconnected and believe that you're no longer in love. Therefore, counteracting cortisol by creating more oxytocin, the love and connection hormone, can make you feel more connected and increase trust and a sense of safety—qualities that may have been lost through trauma.

You can prompt your body to produce oxytocin in various ways. One way is simply through giving and receiving appreciation, particularly with a partner (see the next exercise). Other ways include simple physical contact—such as holding hands, hugging, and other forms of physical affection—warm eye contact, smiling and laughing with others, and sending loving messages to one another. All of these add "love fuel" to your fire and make your relationships more juicy and loving.

Appreciating Each Other

It may sound almost too simple, but giving and receiving appreciation from a partner can be a helpful tool for learning to trust and focus on the positive, particularly because people often focus overly on the negative in the aftermath of trauma. Paying attention to each other, complimenting each other, and recognizing each other even for small things introduces happiness and reconnection into any relationship. Such acknowledgments are especially important in a relationship that has suffered due to PTSD.

Bearing in mind that appreciation has such a strong positive impact on relationships, work with your partner to share three specific appreciations with each other every day before bedtime. This will force both of you to look for something positive in the other, and move you away from focusing on the negative. This can also help you learn to take and give compliments if you are not used to doing so.

Practicing gratitude for the people you care about—either privately or by sharing your appreciation to the other person or even more openly—can boost the part of the brain that produces dopamine and lift your mood. This is the same neurotransmitter that some pharmaceutical antidepressants aim to increase as well. Try telling your partner or someone else how much they inspired you, how much you appreciate them for something they have done.

Expressing Disagreement

Disagreements and disappointments happen in all relationships, it's unreasonable to expect not to have any. While it may seem more peaceful not to talk about conflict, avoiding talking about issues can actually create more intractable relationship problems in the long run. Conflict usually builds up, to surface later in a much more intensified form. Talking about issues in the moment can prevent explosions of feelings later. Not talking about difficulties—swallowing them down—can create distance as well as resentment and disappointment. In contrast, resolving conflicts can eventually bring greater closeness.

Many people, however, don't know where to start. They may lack role models for talking about conflict, not know how to resolve differences, and/or be afraid of tackling problems. The challenge is to change your perspective on conflict, so that you don't avoid conflict, but instead learn how to address problems and move beyond them. With a few tools, resolving disagreements can become easier than you might think.

Camilla was concerned that if she told her partner about her feelings and expectations then she would have to do so with everyone else, too. The idea was overwhelming. She realized that she had never really addressed any conflict before, because it hadn't been safe to as a child. Camilla explained that as a child she had been punished for expressing her needs and asking that they be met. Doing so now would highlight not having done so in the past, bringing sadness and grief.

What if it was safe to have a disagreement and have your needs met? What if you knew you would still be loved, that you wouldn't feel overwhelmed or as if you were a burden? Let's put addressing conflict into practice.

Handling Conflicts Successfully

Address conflicts as soon as possible. The longer you wait, the more charged the topic can become. That said, trauma survivors often have delayed emotional reactions. If this is the case for you, explain to your partner that you may not always be aware in the moment when something bothers you. With time and safety, you will get better at this. Use the following tips to help grow your conflict skills.

- When you express disagreement or dislikes or try to resolve a conflict, begin by feeling your feet on the floor. Bring your attention to the sensations in your body. What is

your body telling you? If your body is tensing up and emotions rise to the surface, name and observe your feelings.
- Try holding hands and looking into each other's eyes while working to resolve a disagreement. This can prevent both of you from going into defense mode and can make it easier to feel supported, safe, and loved. Be aware that you want to speak from your heart and not from your fear. Try to observe your fear, anger, disappointment, or other emotions with kindness.
- Perhaps start by saying, "Listen, there's something I'd like to talk to you about. Would now be a good time?"
- Convey your distress without blame. Use "I" statements instead of "you" accusations. When we start a sentence with "you did this" or "you did that," the other person's automatic response is usually to be defensive or put up a wall. "I" statements have a much better chance of being heard and understood (Rogers 1959).

- Practice stating one request at a time, such as: "I feel uncomfortable when you do this and I would feel better if you could do that." Try to avoid discussing a laundry list of complaints or going back too far into the past. Doing so quickly becomes overwhelming. It's hard to resolve everything at once—stay with one issue at a time. When you've successfully resolved one disagreement, you're far more likely to tackle the next one successfully as well. Don't forget to check your nervous system. When you and your partner are both ready, then you can address the next issue.
- Before you respond to your partner, pause and breathe, so that you feel calm and your emotions don't take over when your partner disagrees with you (Scurlock-Durana 2017). Reflect back what you heard and how you interpret what has been said: "What I see is _____, and how I interpret that is _____." Now check if what you see and how you interpret the situation is how your partner sees it (Rogers 1959). Do

you both understand it in the same way?
- If you're triggered, pause. Wait until you feel calmer to discuss the issue again. If you need to stop, inform your partner that you need to take a break. You could say something like, "Give me a moment, I need to gather my thoughts."
- Practice empathy and compassion with both yourself and your partner when a misunderstanding occurs. Be patient with yourself and your partner. Your partner may need help to understand the traumatic reactions that arise during conflict.

***

In a long-term relationship, it's impossible to avoid having to express differences at some point. Every time you make an honest effort to communicate your feelings and address conflict—at home, work, or play—you will gain more confidence and skill. This is true even if you aren't honored, respected, or heard in the way you want to be. When resolving conflict fails, look back to see what you can learn from it. Step by step, you are on your way to handling the next difference that arises better.

The goal is to have nonjudgmental and loving communication. This allows openness, a sense of safety, and emotional intimacy. Such communication isn't about winning, it's about resolving conflict. This requires skills. However, if both partners practice these techniques, both can feel safer and better understood. Isn't that worth a try?

Claiming Your Space

Boundaries are direct or indirect claims to your own physical, emotional, psychological, and energetic space; they're about distinguishing between yourself and another. Physical boundaries aren't walls, but rather simple spatial claims, such as the distance between yourself and another that you preserve. Emotional boundaries involve considering your own emotional needs, saying yes or no, and asserting your own likes and dislikes. Psychological boundaries focus on your thoughts and deciding when and how much of what you're thinking is appropriate to share.

Many abuse survivors have difficulty knowing what exactly boundaries are. As a result, abuse survivors can be insecure and lack the necessary knowledge to set boundaries. It's not always easy to establish appropriate boundaries after they have been repeatedly crossed, for example, through physical, emotional, or sexual abuse or harassment. You may have learned to submit, to please without considering your needs, to give but not be allowed to receive—and to give up or sacrifice your needs in hopes of experiencing less conflict or pain, or simply in order to survive. You may have learned to believe that others have authority over your body and your mind. You may not only have had to give up your desires, you may have been conditioned to think that you don't have rights, such as the right to say yes or no. As a result, you will say yes when you mean no, smile when you are in pain, do things that you don't want to do, overextend, or over share. Over time, these sacrifices can build into resentment, a sense of feeling burdened or burnt out, depression and anxiety, and much more. Please let me emphasize: You have the right to say yes, no, and maybe. It's both okay and healthy to set boundaries.

I borrowed the following exercise from Marjory Rand (Rand and Fewster 2015), one of the founders of integrative body psychotherapy (IBP). Many of my clients initially misjudge the extent of the positive outcomes this exercise can have. This is a much more powerful exercise than you might think. Setting your boundaries and knowing that they are respected—by you and the other person, even if you need to be insistent—can foster trust, safety, and a feeling of being grounded. Do this exercise first by yourself. When you are ready, do it with your partner. If your partner isn't willing to try it, imagine your partner's presence. You'll need yarn.

Sensing Your Boundaries

1. Sit on the floor and create a circle around you with yarn. Consciously choose what kind of yarn you want, what color, what width, and so on.
2. Notice how wide or narrow the circle is around you. Is there equal space between you and the yarn everywhere? (There's no wrong or right way of doing this exercise; we're all individuals.)
3. As you look at the yarn, what are you aware of in your body? Your sensations may prompt you to adjust the yarn. You can do as much as you want or not.
4. Tell yourself: This space is Mine; others can come into My circle only if they are invited and only with My permission. You may decide that nobody can come into your circle. That is perfectly fine and your right. Observe your physical reactions again. What sensations do you become aware of?

5. After you have practiced this exercise for a few weeks by yourself, practice it with your partner. This time, sit in front of your partner on the floor and create a circle around you. Have your partner do the same. Notice if your yarn overlaps. Do you feel guilty or scared that your partner isn't in your circle, or vice versa? Is your circle far away from your partner's circle? Let this inform you where your boundaries are, but don't criticize yourself. You are only making an observation.

***

Learning, knowing, and honoring your boundaries may feel awkward, frightening, or impossible, but not doing so will result in unhappiness and difficulty. Like so much of life, practice can make this easier and more familiar. The rewards along the way will encourage you to continue. Know that, while at first, both you and others may have to adjust to your new behavior of setting boundaries, as you keep doing it, others will become used to it. People who are able to have a healthy dynamic with you will respect you for setting boundaries and knowing yourself well.

Finding Support

No matter what kind of trauma you experienced, the strong reactions of PTSD can be challenging for yourself and others to cope with. These challenges can cause disconnects between you and your partner, friends, family, and community. You may have already become isolated or estranged as a result. Building a support system that helps you reconnect not only to your partner but also to people outside your relationship can speed your recovery and restore your sense of safety and security.

Sometimes, asking for support can be difficult because it can tap into feelings of helplessness and powerlessness. What if, though, you become *more* powerful by being supported? What if support *adds* to your strength rather than takes away from it? Asking for support can also seem daunting because you may not know how to convey to someone else what you need, and others may not understand right away difficulties they've never experienced. You may be surprised. Others can feel better knowing that there is something they can do. And if they're not capable of learning to be there for you, at least you can try to show them how—often we don't even attempt this. Regardless of the outcome, asking for support is a good opportunity to practice acknowledging your needs and expressing them to others.

It can help to educate family and friends about PTSD so they have some understanding of what someone with trauma may be going through; this may help them not to take your reactions personally. Many family members and friends want to help but don't know how. They may simply not know what you need.

Andrew explained to me with frustration that his mother gave him a lot of advice and suggestions. Although she meant well, she was unknowingly exacerbating Andrew's shame about having PTSD. I asked him to focus on what kind of support he wanted instead and then to try enrolling his parents and friends in a different approach to supporting him. He wanted, he said, to be validated—to have a cheerleader when he felt hopeless and down. He needed to feel that someone would be on his side. He decided to discuss this with his mom so that he wouldn't avoid her and further isolate himself.

You may want to ask others to assist you with small acts of care, such as by making phone calls, running errands, or helping you find therapeutic resources. You're not lazy. Nor do you have less intelligence. You just can't access certain parts of the brain when your trauma is activated. Remember: the nervous system overrides logic. As a result, trauma survivors can have a hard time being logical and can easily become overwhelmed.

Rebecca admitted that she has a tendency to withdraw. She needed her friends to reach out to her during the times she did. I suggested that she try to educate her friends, saying something like, "I tend to withdraw, but I would really like to stay connected. I wonder if you could help by calling me or reaching out to me at such times—would that be possible?" As a lopsided friendship isn't ideal over the long run, when Rebecca was feeling better, she could then reach out more again.

There are those who never ask for any help, and those who are afraid to seek professional help and so lean heavily on friends and family. Try to take a balanced approach in terms of receiving support from the people around you. Consider receiving additional help from a psychotherapist, group therapy, or online groups. The following exercise will help you practice allowing support to enter your life.

What Does Support Feel Like?

1. First, feel the chair or the surface you are sitting on.
2. Notice how the chair is supporting your body.
3. Lean against the back of the chair more heavily and then less heavily. What do you observe?

4. Check in with your senses: is your body relaxing or constricting?
5. Tell yourself: I am supported by the chair in this moment. Do you feel powerless or helpless because your body is supported? Probably not. You don't have to feel powerless when your partner, family, or friend supports you either.
6. Do this exercise every day for three weeks for just a few minutes. In the first week, look around on a daily basis and see how you may be supported but have never noticed.
7. In the second week, try sitting back to back with your partner, or a friend who is willing to do this exercise with you. Lean against your partner, feeling the physical support. Lean more heavily and then less heavily. Notice what your body and mind tell you about this interaction. Reverse the exercise and let your partner lean against you. Tell your partner when to stop. Do this exercise 3 to 5 times.

8. In the third week, do a visualization exercise in which you imagine a partner or friend supporting you in new, different ways. What kind of support can you allow yourself to receive? How does your body react this time? If you feel tension, focus on the tension and follow it until it shifts.

When you're comfortable, ask for a small act of support. Slowly work toward something bigger.

When There Is No Family Support: Estrangement

PTSD can cause so much disconnect that it can lead to estrangement. When, by choice or not, we no longer interact or communicate with a family member or other formerly close person, we have become estranged. Also referred to as an "emotional cut-off," estrangement describes the process by which people separate from their family, friends, and others by creating physical and emotional distance to reduce or eliminate trauma triggers (Bowen 1966). Unfortunately, estrangement from family members can at times exacerbate PTSD's effects because for many people, family serves as a basic source of support.

One reason for the loss of contact with others can be attempts to avoid PTSD triggers. You may be easily irritated, upset, overwhelmed, or sensitive to sounds, such as the voices of others. Melissa confided that after her stroke all she wanted was to sit in a quiet space and stare at nothing. Every interaction with others seemed just too much.

Unfortunately, adult survivors of childhood abuse often don't have adequate help from their family. Parents may have abandoned you, or perhaps they were and are so abusive that contact with them brings up too many memories or is too difficult, dangerous, or unhealthy.

Dianna was estranged from her father. She had to sever all contact with him because he wouldn't stop emotionally abusing her. Her father was charming to everyone else and didn't abuse her in front of others. As a result, nobody believed her or her mother—friends and family members kept telling him Dianna's whereabouts and trying to convince her that she should have contact with him and "make things right." Once her father found her again, he would return to stalking her, calling and sending letters, only to further emotionally abuse her. When Dianna's friends or other family members wouldn't tell him her new phone number or address, he would steal her number from their phones when they left the room. The only way to make sure her father couldn't find her was to break all contacts they had in common. Dianna and her mother lost most of their support system this way, leaving them lonely, isolated, and mistrusting of people's loyalty.

Michael was abandoned by his father when he was eleven years old. His father estranged *him.* In Michael's words, "He went into the Navy during World War II. And then I never saw him for twenty-two years. He never returned home. And it was good riddance, you know. I didn't have to put up with his abuse anymore."

It's important to note that, although estrangement is common in dysfunctional families, not everyone who is estranged from their family was abused or had a dysfunctional family.

Attempting Reconciliation

A reader of my blog once asked if we have to keep a door open for our abusive parents to reconnect. You don't have to. Only you can determine whether or not you want to. Only you know the limits of your pain and triggers. Certainly, you always need to make sure you are safe, physically and emotionally. If you do wish to reconnect, the former abuser needs to accept your boundaries and not hurt you anymore. If you decide you want to try to rebuild a former abusive relationship, know that the other person may not have changed. It's important to make sure you aren't the only one working on the relationship.

Despite the abuse in their past, as an adult Michael longed for a connection with his father and decided to hire a private detective to track him down.

The detective located two possible addresses for him. Rather than calling, Michael decided to drive to one of the houses and knock on the door. His father answered, smelling of alcohol, and didn't know who Michael was. As they talked, it became clear to Michael that his father hadn't changed. Michael saw him a few more times: each time his father was drunk, only talked about himself, and asked for money. This time it was Michael's decision to estrange his father. Cutting the cords, Michael never saw his father again. For Michael, on some level it was useful to see his father's "old self." As he explained, "It helped in an obtuse way even though at first it was terribly disappointing."

I have witnessed reconciliation attempts that have had successful outcomes and those that have not. Many of my clients have reported that they tried to confront their abusers, but the abusers either did not remember their abusive actions or claimed they were made up. However, sometimes reconciliation is possible. Although a lot of anger and sadness may come to the surface during the healing process, it is possible to have a relationship again. For one of the readers of my blog, after ten years of counseling and working with her formerly abusive mother, she found herself able to appreciate and even love her mother again.

Everyone is entitled to their own opinion and their own path. Nobody can tell you what your path is. However, if you're considering reconciliation, it's a good idea to be prepared for what can happen when you try to reconcile.

When you are ready and it is safe for you to reconcile, the first step to reconciliation is forgiveness. Forgiveness is not about making abuse okay or giving someone an excuse, it is about realizing and acknowledging a person's limitations and flaws, so that you can let go of your anger, sadness, or other emotions. In this sense, forgiveness is for you, not the other.

Michael was able to forgive because he understood his father's weaknesses and how his father had been shaped by his own traumatic history of abandonment and abuse to become who he was. Michael also stopped having expectations of his father. As a psychologist himself, he knew that some parents (not all) treat their children as they themselves were treated because they had no healthy role models and never healed or corrected their own behavior. Forgiveness for Michael meant not holding on to his story anymore and coming to terms with what his father was capable of and what he wasn't.

The knowledge that abuse can be passed on upsets some of my clients and readers—they fear that others could suspect them of being a possible abuser just because they have experienced trauma. Please do not see trauma outcomes only in black or white. Trauma impacts and shapes us all differently. Just because it impacts one person a certain way doesn't mean it will cause the same behavior in another or in everyone. This doesn't mean *you* have turned out this way, or that other people see you in this light. For example, unlike his father, Michael has always been kind and compassionate despite the abuse he endured.

Make a Reconciliation Plan

Rebuilding an estranged relationship can sometimes help heal old wounds and prompt new feelings of belonging and joy. The endeavor can at times be overwhelming or upsetting. Making a reconciliation plan can help you prepare yourself psychologically for such challenges.

- Be prepared: what are possible negative and positive outcomes of reconciling?
- Check in with yourself: are you ready to reconcile, or are you attempting to reconcile only because the other person requested it and you question your own actions in the estrangement?
- Set your intention, but try not to have high expectations for reconnecting with the estranged person.
- You are never responsible for being abused. Sort out what issues aren't yours and be aware that past trauma patterns may set you up for taking inappropriate responsibility; for example, blaming yourself when

it was not your fault, or thinking you could have done something differently.
- Be patient. If the relationship is safe, give it time to develop again.
- Try to recognize how the other person is or isn't trying to be there for you.
- Know, keep, and set your physical and emotional boundaries.
- Set rules for your boundaries. "There is no (touch, cussing, alcohol, etc.); otherwise you leave."
- Each time you connect with the formerly estranged individual, evaluate if this is healthy for you.
- If this doesn't work, don't beat yourself up. Instead, be proud that you tried.

***

I Thought We'd Never Speak Again: The Road from Estrangement to Reconciliation (2002) by Laura Davis offers helpful advice on managing the details of the reconciliation process, such as how to write a reconciliation letter. Davis also offers ongoing support at www.lauradavis.net.

Surrogate Parents

When reconciliation with a family member isn't an option, support can come from people who feel like family. Now and then we have the opportunity to—informally or formally—adopt other people as surrogate parents or soul siblings. Michael was fortunate to have an older couple in his life who served that purpose. The three of them shared interests in playing music and organized jam sessions in the couple's home when Michael was a college student. Over the years, they frequently spent time together, and stayed in touch after he moved away. It was always a very healing and rewarding relationship for him.

If you can't reconcile with estranged family and don't have any surrogate family, begin to build your own support system by establishing or strengthening friendships and perhaps hiring professional support.

Professional Support

If you are a trauma survivor or are close to someone who suffers from the aftermath of trauma, there are many avenues for support. Individual therapy, support groups, couples therapy, and trauma rehab can all help you understand the feelings and behaviors that are associated with your trauma and move toward healing. Various nonprofit organizations—as well as some schools with psychology programs—offer therapy for a very low fee. Some individual therapists offer sliding fee scales or work pro bono. For some kinds of trauma, your state or local government may offer free or low-cost support. For example, in California, victims of crimes can receive therapy for free from the state's Victims of Crime Compensation Program, provided they meet the program requirements. So even if money is scarce, professional resources may be available. Support can also come in the form of reading books or watching videos on a topic.

Conclusion: The Path from Disconnect to Connection

Withdrawal due to depression or anxiety—and related feelings of disconnect and emotional distance—is a common PTSD symptom that can interfere in relationships. It doesn't have to be this way. By learning to communicate about conflict and triggers and to convey love and appreciation, you can renew bonds and intimacy and rebuild a sense of safety. Support is essential during this time, whether that is from a partner, family or surrogate family, friends, or professionals. Practicing communication and finding support, either within or outside existing relationships, can help you lay the foundation for a trauma-resilient relationship in your future. Start wherever you feel most comfortable and take one step at a time.

CHAPTER 6

Overcoming Financial and Career Barriers

"May your choices reflect your hopes, not your fears."
—Nelson Mandela

This chapter aims to help you identify professional and financial barriers created by your traumatic experiences. It offers ways to eliminate or reduce these, so that you can be the powerful person you truly are—able to achieve your personal goals, large and small, today and in the future.

Whether or not you have experienced trauma related to your work or finances, any type of trauma can cause you to struggle with issues such as job performance, career choices, motivation, and achieving success, however you define it. You may also face money problems, such as debt, overspending or hoarding money, or procrastinating in paying bills.

Surprisingly, these problems may be rooted in your physiology and in your underlying fears and beliefs, conscious or unconscious—all of these are affected by the trauma in your life.

If you feel ashamed about struggling with these issues, please know that many people wrestle with similar problems. Typically, people lack effective tools and knowledge about these kinds of chronic problems. You don't have to—I've written this chapter to give you more tools and knowledge to help you overcome such barriers.

The Body's Barriers to Success: Fight, Flight, Freeze

Remember, when you experience stress and trauma, the logical mind is hijacked by the body's nervous system. As a result, the body's survival mode—your fight, flight, or freeze response—dictates your behavior in all areas of your life. This includes career, money, and success. Your body does what it does in order for you to feel and be safe again. However, at some point, it needs to exit survival mode and return to resting mode. In terms of your career or finances, being stuck in fight, flight, or freeze mode may look like one of the following.

Fight

Typical fight reactions include anger, blaming others or yourself, and creating drama at work or home to gain adrenaline. For example, you may blame your colleagues, boss, or someone else for your lack of success or dissatisfaction with your career or financial situation. You may also direct your anger inward, beating yourself up about choices you made. Further, research has shown that people sometimes blame others for bad investment advice or judge family members for their spending habits as tactics to reduce their own anxiety (Klontz and Klontz 2009).

Flight

When your nervous system is stuck in flight mode, you may have a tendency to run away from stressors, to quit or change, whether that's changing investments, banks, or your job. You may hoard money or store excessive food just in case "something happens," as was common during and after the Great Depression (Klontz and Klontz 2009) as well as after wars and natural disasters.

Freeze

The freeze reaction can cause you to become easily overwhelmed and unable to start or finish anything. You may lack motivation, procrastinate, or deny opportunities that come along. Given the goals you want to achieve, your behavior probably doesn't make rational sense. This state of the "frozen" nervous system, however, is about being still and avoiding action. Therefore, you may not address money issues by not paying or looking at your bills or failing to invoice clients (Klontz and Klontz 2009).

Remember: such behaviors are usually governed not by the logical mind but by the nervous system still in trauma mode. Unfortunately, many people try to self-medicate these feelings and may seek to soothe themselves in unhealthy ways, such as by shopping or abusing drugs or alcohol. At first, this can feel good. It's half-joke and half-truth to say you need "retail therapy." However, if you have to keep calming your nervous system and painful emotions this way, anxiety resulting from accumulating debts will soon catch up with you.

There are healthier, more sustainable ways to soothe your nervous system. (You can still shop, just try not to do so for the wrong reasons.) Start by checking in with yourself when you make a purchase, are looking at your bills, or are at work. What do you feel in your body? What emotions do you experience? Are you in survival mode? If so, make a list of soothing techniques that have worked for you in the past and that you can apply now (see "Taming Your Nervous System" in chapter 2 for suggestions). Have this list easily available: you may not be able to remember these techniques as readily when your logical mind has been hijacked. Once you've soothed your nervous system, assess if you still want to react the same way. Do you now want to make a different choice?

Barrier: Fear of Change

Another source of activation for the nervous system can be fear of change. Whether you are considering a new career, a new investment possibility, a new routine, or anything else, the idea of change can be frightening. Such fear can come from many different events or circumstances and can surface as different threats for different people. For example, it can mean that we have to face the unknown, or that we have to shift away from our safe routine and what feels familiar. For a trauma survivor, the fear of being unsafe and the need for predictability are often at the forefront of every action.

The steps we lay out to accomplish change are often just too big. This can be overwhelming. Thus, when we take bigger steps and more risks, we may activate the part of the brain called the amygdala, which signals our nervous system to go into fight-flight-freeze mode. The larger the steps we take toward change, the more fear we create—as a result, we may feel blocked from doing anything. In *One Small Step Can Change Your Life: The Kaizen Way* (2004), psychologist Robert Maurer suggests taking smaller, easily achievable steps, in alignment with the Japanese technique known as *kaizen*. Small steps give you a better chance of bypassing the amygdala and connecting instead with the cortex, the logical-thought part of the brain.

The more gradual the steps we take, the less fear and anxiety we experience. In return, we feel more encouraged as we move on to the next task. This can ultimately lead to success. Trauma survivors have especially strong reactions when the amygdala is activated because the amygdala holds our existing traumatic memories. Because these traumatic memories may attach to anything that appears to have similarities, trauma survivors may quickly feel intensely overwhelmed—frequently disproportionately so. As we don't want the nervous system to go into survival mode unnecessarily, taking smaller steps can be critical.

Accomplishing one small step at a time can give you the confidence and courage to keep going. For example, when I decided to write this book, I was overwhelmed at times. I had to figure out small steps I could take. Sometimes I felt so anxious that I would encourage myself, "Just write one paragraph," or, "Read one page of a research paper." I kept telling myself that I only had to figure out the next phrase and then see where the words led. What's your first step? How can you make that step even smaller and more manageable? This approach may not take you to your goal as fast as you want, but ultimately it can get you there—a much better outcome than being discouraged or defeated by feeling overwhelmed. What does taking a small step look like for you?

In our society, we are often led to believe that the bigger the steps we take and the bigger the goals we set, the more accomplished we are. Such a belief prompts shame and guilt when we don't do this. It can be helpful to shift your perspective and try on a view that smaller steps can lead to bigger steps. Success is about achieving smaller goals that can lead to grand ones.

Because big steps can overwhelm you and cue your nervous system, in the following exercise, I offer suggestions for breaking down big steps into smaller ones. This will move you toward accomplishing your goals. The point is to create change while allowing your brain to stay calm.

Take Small Steps for Bigger Changes

1. Begin by laying out the steps necessary to achieve a goal of your choice.
2. Next, break each step toward your goal into smaller steps.
3. Now, think of the first small step and see if your body reacts to it or not. To do this, find a comfortable place to sit or lie down and then visualize the step—silently or aloud—and

observe your sensations. When your body agrees with a step, you may feel an expansion; when it doesn't, you may feel contraction. If your body is tensing up, the step may need to be even smaller.
4. If the step needs to be smaller, break it down even further, then test it again by checking in with your body. Are you feeling lighter and more expansive? Great! You've figured out your first step and gotten the green light from your nervous system.
5. Take the first step toward your goal and praise and applaud yourself for taking it, even if you still have a long way to go. You can get there!

Barrier: Fear of Success

Unfortunately, for people suffering the long-term effects of trauma, excitement can also trigger a fight, flight, or freeze reaction, telling the brain that success is something to be alarmed about. Isn't success a good thing? Not when the body associates excitement with fear. The act of realizing a hope or dream is exciting; that excitement can cue fear. A little nervousness with success is normal, but for trauma survivors, this can specifically trigger feelings of anxiety. Those feelings can overwhelm any positive feelings, filling you only with a desire for the fear to disappear. Readers have written to me about their bodies feeling terribly tense and unhappy when they experience success—and as a result, pushing themselves to not feel happy or good.

Fear isn't a bad thing. In fact, fear is a vital alarm system that prods us to determine if we are in danger or not. If so, it urges us to seek safety. In fear mode, the heart speeds up, breathing becomes more rapid, blood pressure rises, and the body releases hormones to prepare us to react. The physiological response to excitement is very similar. Unfortunately, once we have experienced anything traumatic, the body can misinterpret physiological arousal states such as excitement and happiness and translate them as warning signals. The message becomes: "Wait a second, I recognize that fast heartbeat and adrenaline—I must be scared." Immediately, the nervous system will activate survival mode to make sure that this time we are safe.

Do you fear success? Have you noticed yourself deferring or dismissing compliments? When you imagine being successful, are you able to stay with that thought or do you immediately think about something else or criticize yourself? Do you react positively to success, or do you feel bad or guilty? If you answered yes to any of these questions, try the following exercise to help align your body's nervous system with success. This exercise was introduced on my *Psychology Today* blog in 2011 to help readers address fear of success and similar obstacles; I've updated it for this book. The exercise will help your body avoid confusing excitement with fear, so that you can move toward success joyfully.

Sync Your Body to Success

1. Make a list of past accomplishments that you connect positive feelings with, related to your job, hobbies, health, home, or any other areas.
2. If you can't come up with anything, try looking for smaller successes that evoke pleasant memories. Maybe you increased your running from 5 to 10 minutes. Maybe you ate one healthy meal a day versus previously eating none.
3. Think of one accomplishment from your list. What sensations do you feel? Describe your internal sensations with as much detail as you can. Stay with the sensation. You may find that negative emotions and sensations occur. If so, stay with those feelings. Be a curious observer until they shift and you feel relaxed. This may take a few minutes.
4. Now imagine being successful and accomplishing your current goals in the near future. Think about

how you want to feel, how you want to celebrate or be celebrated when your goals are achieved.

5. Stop now, be gentle with yourself, and let this information settle in.

Every time you do this exercise, you can gain more awareness about which sensations are linked with which emotions. For example, is success associated with fear or excitement? Each time you pay attention to your sensations, you are increasing your own body-oriented vocabulary, improving your ability to recognize and describe sensations. With these tools, your body can learn to differentiate between excitement and fear, between one fear and another, and to shift away from negative emotions and sensations. Most people are able to differentiate and describe emotions such as sad, frustrated, angry, and so on, but may not be used to paying attention to or describing sensations (other than hot or cold) in precise terms—for example, pulsing pain, tugging muscle strains, dull ache, and so on. Remember: the language of sensations is the best language you can use to connect with your nervous system when it needs to find calmness.

Another technique for soothing the nervous system and its intense emotional responses is called Emotional Freedom Technique (EFT). EFT involves gently tapping on meridians used in traditional acupuncture; the practice incorporates neurolinguistic programming as well as thought field technique (Craig 2009). Tapping is a way to soothe your body and emotions and lower your stress hormones. You can learn it online for free (for example, see http://www.EFTUniverse.com). Don't worry, it's not complicated. Many people find EFT very strange at first ("How can *this* help me?"), but after trying it, are surprised to find that their anxiety or other negative emotions are reduced and they feel more positive.

Although Catherine was very successful in her career and had an abundant flow of money, she felt unable to open envelopes with invoices in them. She felt too anxious and frozen to make payments, and so they piled up on her desk. Creditors called her constantly and her credit score was very low, but nothing could motivate her to deal with the bills. When I asked her to rate her problem from 1 to 10, she replied that it was a 10 and then some. To lower her anxiety and ease her nervous system, I taught her an EFT exercise. This helped her to pay one bill at a time. Ideally it will help you when your nervous system seems to keep you from the things you want or need to do.

EFT exercises typically take only a few minutes and can be used for any feeling, emotion, behavior, goal, craving, or pain. You can use this simple tapping technique every day. While EFT doesn't appeal to everyone, nearly all of my clients who try it have shown significant improvement. It is easy to find online and free and quick to try! If your nervous system is causing you to feel scared, overwhelmed, angry, or anxious, try using this tapping exercise to lessen the intensity of those feelings.

Trauma Impacting Work

Trauma symptoms can cause you to struggle with concentration and memory loss, learning new skills, problem solving, and other cognitive functions. Trauma can also make it easy for you to become easily overwhelmed, oversensitive or hypervigilant, and sleep deprived (due to insomnia). Further, negative associations and flashbacks can lead to avoiding going to work. All of these can have negative impacts on your career and income.

No matter the original source of the trauma, you can make it easier to be at work by creating a soothing environment or "work sanctuary" (Hughes, Lusk, and Strause 2016). The following exercise can help you do exactly that, through evaluating and improving your workspace. This will allow you to maximize your potential and stay calm.

Create a Trauma-Soothing Work Environment

To increase concentration and memory, try these strategies:
- Ask coworkers not to interrupt you; instead, arrange certain times of

the day that you will be available for them.
- Inquire if you can have a flexible work schedule; this can allow you to work when it's calmer and there are fewer interruptions, or to come in later if you need extra time at home in the morning due to your insomnia.
- Make a list of what to do if you feel triggered at work. For example, you could deactivate intense feelings by conscious breathing, finding a soothing object to look at, etc. Post your list anywhere you are likely to see it often in your workspace.
- Develop a system you can use when you lack concentration, such as double-checking your work before you turn it in, or having someone else check it.
- Use reminders for deadlines, events, and important to-do items. For example, you might add reminders to a calendar, notepad, or phone app, or use voice recordings. Check your list frequently.

To reduce feeling easily overwhelmed or hypersensitive, try these strategies:

- Take breaks on a regular basis.
- Listen to soothing music; consider getting a water fountain for its calming sounds.
- If you are sensitive to noise at work or suffer from hyperacusis—intolerance of seemingly normal sounds, such as shuffling papers or using a computer keyboard—try wearing a sound-cancelling headset and/or using sound-absorption panels, partitions, or a white-noise machine; you may want to try to get an office to yourself.
- Have plants and as much natural light as possible in your workspace.
- Keep your desk clean and organize your office so that it functions well.
- Keep reminders of your life outside the office nearby. For example, place a picture of your family, friends, pets, or your last vacation on your desk.
- Divide bigger projects into smaller pieces or manageable steps.
- If you have a dog, you may want to register your dog as an emotional support animal so that

you can bring your canine buddy to the office. If you have traumatic associations with your workplace, such as having been harassed or robbed, having an emotional support animal with you can help you feel calm and protected.

Work-Related Trauma

Work-related trauma can result from being stalked, bullied, abused, harassed, assaulted, robbed, witnessing trauma, being seriously injured on the job, and so on. If you find yourself continuously reminded of the trauma that occurred, you may find it too hard to return to work—where the trauma occurred—and may have had to go on disability. One study showed that only 10 percent of those who were robbed or assaulted at work—for example, taxi drivers, service station attendants, bank agents, and others—were able to return; others needed a gradual return and job modifications (MacDonald et al. 2003).

If you have trouble going back to work or avoid certain situations due to trauma reminders and flashbacks, exposure therapy can help (Joseph and Gray 2008). Exposure therapy builds on the idea that you can reduce a fear by gradually confronting it. For example, if you are a bus driver, your job is in transportation, or you have been in a vehicle accident and avoid driving, you could try just sitting in a vehicle without driving as your first step to confronting your fear. Notice your sensations and follow them until you are calm. While sitting in the parked vehicle, engine off, you can listen to soothing music, talk on the phone with a loved one, or do anything else that is soothing. You can repeat this step until you feel comfortable sitting in the vehicle without driving. In your next steps, you could slowly work toward driving, first in the parking lot for a few days or weeks and then on the streets again. If this exercise seems impossible, you can also confront your fear by imagining what it would take to drive again.

Whatever you are facing, the following exercise can help guide you through gradually overcoming fears to feel safer to return to or be at work. Plan to repeat the exercise as often as you can, each time going longer or more often, even if it is only a minute more each time.

Resolving Trauma Reminders at Work

1. Make a list of activities, places, or objects that you are scared of. Rate your fears on a scale of 1 to 10 and pick the one that is the lowest on the scale to start with.
2. Set your goals. Plan what activities you need to do to accomplish your goals and identify when would be a good time to do them. Break the activities into smaller activities until you feel they are manageable.
3. As you approach the first activity, notice what sensations you feel in your body. Try not to avoid them. Usually, when you stay with your sensations at length, fear will shift, minimize, or become another feeling.
4. Do the activity that you feel uncomfortable with repeatedly until the intensity lowers. How

long were you able to stay with the activity? How often were you able to do it? Rate your fear again. Is it lower for that specific activity than before?

5. Praise yourself for taking this first step, no matter how small you think it is. Take notes on your progress, so that you can see how far you have come and what has helped you. Don't push yourself, let your fears melt away as they need to. Forcing this process can create more anxiety.

6. Incrementally increase the time of the activity, such as from 5 minutes to 10 or whatever feels possible to you.

7. Continue this exercise until you feel you can take on the next activity, and then the next activity, and so on until you are clear of your fears.

The Trauma Helper Syndrome: Secondary Traumatization

When you are in a profession focused on taking care of or rescuing trauma victims, you experience trauma indirectly at work. As a result, you can develop trauma symptoms yourself. Such professionals—including firefighters, police officers, paramedics, disaster relief specialists, psychotherapists and psychiatrists, emergency room nurses and surgeons, and other caregivers—can develop trauma symptoms through witnessing or hearing about someone else who was traumatized, in a life-threatening situation, attempted suicide, or died. This is referred to as secondary traumatization, secondary traumatic stress, vicarious traumatization, or compassion fatigue (Figley 2002; Pearlman and Saakvitne 1996; Stamm 1999).

People who experience secondary trauma describe taking on the victim's symptoms—such as feeling the same headache or having nightmares. Other symptoms include feeling powerless, anxiety, depression, hearing difficulties, and seeing intrusive images of another's trauma (Babbel 2007).

Some mental health professionals use the term "compassion fatigue" rather than "secondary traumatization." Babette Rothschild explains in her book, *Help for the Helper: The Psychophysiology of Compassion Fatigue and Vicarious Traumatization* (2006), that we develop these symptoms as a natural byproduct of our compassion and empathy. She emphasizes the importance of taking care of not only others but also yourself in order to help prevent symptoms from developing and reduce them when they appear. Further, the more helpless you feel, the more likely you may be to develop symptoms (Babbel 2007). This is understandable: Trauma victims often feel helpless; when we try to help them, we can overidentify with them, and their world can become ours. If we are inexperienced with helping others who have severe trauma, we can feel even more helpless. As you work in your field, you will become better at both helping others and yourself.

Unfortunately, if you don't address your own symptoms they can turn into burnout, health issues, or job loss, and start taking over your life. To help yourself, practice self-care techniques that address both your body and your psyche. The following strategies may include some that will work for you.

Trauma Helper Self-Care Techniques

- Learn to differentiate between your feelings and those of the trauma victims you help. To do so, you first have to know what you are feeling. Pay attention to what you feel physically and emotionally during and after your work with trauma victims. Did your sensations and emotions change when you started? What are the emotions and sensations of the people you help? Are theirs the same as yours?
- Get familiar with your body's warning signals—such as sudden pain, dizziness, sleepiness, anxiety,

and feeling overwhelmed—so that you can identify them when they first appear.
- When you start to feel impacted by traumatic events you see or stories you hear, bring your awareness to your emotional and physical feelings.
- Name quietly to yourself the emotions and feelings that you've experienced since you started listening to and empathizing with the other person.
- If you don't feel your body, ground yourself: take a slow breath and feel the connection of your feet on the floor or earth.
- Create and use visual or sensory reminders of the world that exists outside your work helping traumatized people. You might keep a picture of your last vacation on your desk or phone, touch your wedding ring or another special piece of jewelry, or craft a reminder of joyful times.
- Consciously mark the end of your workday. For example, you could switch to different clothing when

you arrive home or create other rituals to signify that you are now in a relaxed mode and a different environment than work.
- Try to have a positive attitude by being curious, practicing gratitude, and keeping a sense of humor.
- Make a list of how you have helped people. Know that, even when a person you helped couldn't be saved, you still helped them. This will keep you from thinking that you didn't make a difference.
- Seek out supervision, peer support, or an expert in your field for advice and to help you process your experience.
- Learn and practice relaxation techniques that you find useful; use the soothing techniques of this book frequently.
- Fill your cup by nurturing yourself. Take a bath, eat a healthy and delicious meal, get a massage, go for a walk, exercise, or do anything else that makes you feel good.
- Make sure you socialize with people who are important to you so that

your world isn't exclusively that of trauma stories.

Conclusion: From Struggling to Thriving

How well you do in your career and with your goals—and even with success in general—can be impacted by your body's trauma mode and your deep-seated beliefs. This doesn't have to be forever. As we will explore in the next chapter, when you sync your body with what you truly want and work to align your beliefs with these goals and dreams, you can thrive in areas where you previously struggled.

CHAPTER 7

Triumphing Over Disempowering Beliefs

"If we could get your subconscious mind to agree with your conscious mind about being happy, that's when your positive thoughts work."
—Bruce Lipton

Trauma may have caused you to have beliefs that make you feel helpless, lead you to distrust others, hinder feeling good about yourself and life, and lessen your motivation. Such beliefs can engender negative thoughts of being damaged and feed negative expectations, such as that you will never have a career or earn enough money, will never be successful, and can't trust anyone (Cox, Resnick, and Kilpatrick 2014). Because they are stored deep within your subconscious, such disempowering beliefs may be driving your decisions and countering your positive affirmations, without you even being aware of them. These beliefs don't have to interfere with your productivity, peace of mind, and enjoyment of life. This chapter brings these limiting beliefs into your consciousness and helps you address them so that you can reclaim your power, trust, desires, and needs.

What Are Beliefs?

Our beliefs aren't necessarily based on facts—rather, they're based on what we have interpreted as facts or have simply been told are true. Such interpretations come from how we make sense of the world around us given the information we have available at that time or age. Most of our beliefs about ourselves, others, and the surrounding world—what are called our core beliefs (Wenzel 2012)—are created during our first six years of childhood and are downloaded as a program into our subconscious (Lipton 2008). This is part of why trauma has more impact on us the younger we are. Beliefs add rigidity to related thoughts, fears, emotions, sensations, and behaviors, making it difficult for us to modify them unless we are aware of the beliefs and consciously work to shift them.

Trauma can introduce negative beliefs and catastrophic thoughts at any age. These thoughts and beliefs will serve as our truth until we become aware that they are untrue and that we need to change them. However, when they have existed for a very long time, we tend not to question them.

Because 95 percent of our actions are directed by the subconscious and only 5 percent by the conscious mind (Szegedy-Maszak 2005), this chapter explores disempowering beliefs common among trauma survivors that may be residing in your subconscious. This chapter also offers exercises to help you question and change these beliefs.

Belief: I Am Powerless and Helpless

If you experienced a traumatic event of any kind, not having been able to stop the trauma from happening may have left you feeling and believing that you are powerless and helpless (Beckham and Beckham 2004). As a result, you may now try really hard to control your environment in hopes that you'll be able to detect when you are in danger. Life, however, teaches us over and over again that we cannot control everything—a lesson that ends up perpetuating in trauma survivors feelings of powerlessness, helplessness, and frustration.

Abuse of any kind has a distinctive impact on feeling and maintaining a sense of being powerless. That sense of powerlessness was created when our boundaries—such as our ability to say no and have it be heard and respected—were violated and/or we were repeatedly punished for expressing our needs. Because you didn't have any power in the past—and it was safer not to appear powerful—you may not be aware that you have power now. Being in the power of the abuser may have made you distrust power in general, including your own. Seeking to become more powerful can thus trigger memories of abuse, continuing the cycle of powerlessness.

No matter how they began, feelings of powerlessness can cause you to focus on comparing yourself with people at work or elsewhere who seem to be more successful or powerful than you (Galinsky, Gruenfeld, and Magee 2003). This can come in the form of asking for advice from colleagues excessively; needing to be validated more than usual by your boss, clients, or customers; feeling inferior; and not trusting your own authority to make decisions. More broadly, feelings of powerlessness can cause us to fear making the wrong decisions, to avoid action due to fear of mistakes, and to let other people be responsible or powerful—and to give up our own dreams and desires more easily.

For many people, having money is having power. The psychological component of feeling powerful versus powerless affects our financial decisions. One study showed that feeling powerful actually increased saving behaviors due to a desire to maintain status and power (Garbinsky, Klesse, and Jennifer

2014). When your subconscious isn't comfortable with feeling powerful, it can be difficult to make and/or save money. A client once told me, "I have plenty of money coming in, but somehow it always disappears and I do not seem to be able to hang on to it." She later realized that she spent all her money in order to subconsciously lessen her power.

We all face challenges and obstacles as we strive for what we want in life—typically goals that make us feel more personal power. Some goals seem to have more barriers than others, but it's up to us how we approach and surmount these barriers. People who suffer from past trauma, however, also face a particular obstacle, one that isn't always recognized: strong limiting beliefs. Through learning to define power for ourselves and to become comfortable being in our own power, we can overcome these limiting beliefs. When you're accustomed to feeling your personal power, you are more confident and competent, aware of your strength, and motivated to fulfill your dreams. This isn't a negative type of power that hurts others. Rather, "This type of power represents a movement toward self-realization and transcendent goals in life; its primary aim is mastery of self, not others" (Firestone and Cattlett 2009, 316).

Your powerlessness, however, may have become so familiar to you that you feel as if you can't shed it now; at the same time, you may judge yourself for not being powerful or successful. But judgments never help anyone—they just extend your sense of powerlessness, make you feel smaller, and delay necessary healing of wounds. Rather, take an active approach to discovering why you don't feel safe enough or confident enough to be powerful. A first step to increasing personal power is recognizing that the belief "I am powerless" can stem from your traumatic experience.

Know that you deserve to be powerful and to shine. Please alter the following statement to what is right for you: "I can learn how to take the next steps to allow, create, and feel safe to enjoy success and power in my life." You may have felt powerless over what happened to you or your loved ones in the past, but now you can focus on where you *do* have power instead of on where you don't. Start by paying attention to where you have the power of choice, even in seemingly mundane activities such as choosing to go for a walk, drive, eat, read, and so on. Go through your day and whenever you make a choice, name it, For example, "I chose to read this book," "I chose to read for an hour," "I chose to put it on my side table." There are many moments in a day that we have a choice over. See which ones you pick to become aware of.

There are other steps you can take to get in touch with your personal power, steps that are not controlled by the mind but the body. Poses and posture, as well as facial expressions and gestures, can make you feel powerful and align your psyche with feeling powerful. For example, when I was about eighteen years old, I chose to express myself through dance. Dancing changed how I was holding myself, lifting not only my posture but also my mood and sense of confidence.

Much later, when studying the work of Stanley Keleman (a pioneer in somatic psychology), I learned that correcting my posture had helped me psychologically: our muscles organize according to our experiences, creating a habitual physical pattern and linking the memory of our emotions to our musculature (Keleman 1981).

Growing up, I was very shy. I felt powerless and looked down all the time, my chest caving in. By holding my posture straight and my gaze up, as dance required, my muscles started to signal different messages to my brain—as a result, my thoughts and emotions began to change. It's actually much harder to feel shy when you walk with your gaze up. Changing my posture caused physiological changes, which in turn improved my thinking, feelings, and behavior. Studies have shown that actions of the body have the capability to change your mind and your behavior; for example, holding open, expansive poses even for just one minute decreased stress hormones such as cortisol and increased testosterone in men; maintaining a concave chest reversed the effect (Carney, Cuddy, and Yap 2010). Changing your posture can help strengthen your sense of power, which in turn boosts your confidence, optimism, performance level, ability to cope with stress, comfort level in terms of risks, and ability to be more present (Carney, Cuddy, and Yap 2010).

To counteract feeling powerless or helpless, I suggest you embody your power, even if you have to pretend at first. (Fake it until you make it!) Practice the following exercise on a regular basis to create a body memory and become more familiar with the new feelings. You can then use this exercise before any situation where you want to feel more confident and grounded, such as public speaking or a job interview.

Embody Your Personal Power

1. Sit on a chair. Notice how you are sitting. Is your body straight or hunched over? What are your physical sensations at this moment? What are your emotions?

2. In small increments, lean back on your chair and open your chest, lifting your chin and gaze. With each small increase, pause and check what you feel in your body. Your body needs to reorganize habitual patterns; if you feel uncomfortable at first, try to be patient.
3. Now, can you make yourself even bigger? Stretch your neck and widen your shoulders. Hold this posture for a minute or two. What do you notice now? Does your throat feel more open? Do you breathe differently? Do your eyes see something different than before?
4. Feel your feet strong and solid on the ground and imitate a posture of confidence, pushing your chest out and up. Even if this feels uncomfortable in the beginning, keep doing it until your body accepts this posture and becomes more familiar with it.

Belief: I Can't Trust Anyone or Anything

After a traumatic event, a survivor often thinks of the worst scenario all the time and feels that no person or situation can be trusted or is safe. For example, after Craig's wife died in a car accident, Craig no longer trusted other drivers and feared that his children and other family members could never be safe in a car. Such worries and negative expectations—known as intrusive rumination—can become repetitive and consuming for long stretches of time.

Intrusive thoughts can include distrust toward ourselves as well as toward others and the world around us. We may blame ourselves because something happened in the past at a time when we couldn't count on our instinct or abilities to protect us. We may have a falsified sense of self and blame ourselves or others for our trauma symptoms or not being able to recover from the trauma (American Psychological Association 2013). Craig blamed himself, thinking that somehow he could have done something to save his wife. If you or someone close to you were harmed or died in a transportation accident, shooting, natural disaster, or other trauma, you may wonder how you can ever trust that you or your loved ones are safe. Unfortunately, the more you think this way, the deeper the trauma symptoms, PTSD, and depression can penetrate into your psyche and body (Ehlers and Clark 2000).

Your disempowering belief may perpetuate a sense of impending threat, whether it is a hazard to your safety, health, happiness, or anything else. There are steps you can take to loosen the grip of beliefs. Knowing and acknowledging that these beliefs, thoughts, and fears may be a byproduct of trauma is the first step to overcoming their hold on you. The second step is challenging them. Ask yourself: from 0 to 10, how likely is it to really happen? The third step is to visualize what you want to happen instead and ask yourself, "How can I think about this situation differently?" Ask yourself this question several times in a row until you feel you begin to see more positive choices.

Studies have shown that thinking about positive changes that may also have stemmed from the traumatic event—known as deliberate rumination (Helgeson, Reynolds, and Tomich 2006)—can actually bring positive meaning to your life, what's called trauma growth (Cann et al. 2010; Taku et al. 2009).

The following exercise gives direction to your undirected, intrusive thoughts by signaling to your body and psyche that you have a plan in place to generate more constructive thoughts. This is a way to begin to recover—or discover—trust in your own mind and body. This technique of addressing intrusive thoughts comes from cognitive therapy and can decrease your fears and PTSD. Here I incorporate the body to make it truly a mind-body exercise. Please be assured: It's normal to have fears. The only way out is to work through them. This doesn't happen overnight. It's a gradual process, so please be patient with yourself and don't give up. We learn to trust by slowly trusting again.

Discover Trust

1. Engage your uncontrollable thoughts by developing a plan. What plan could help you to prevent something fearful from occurring or a fearful situation from worsening? Depending on your specific fears, you might develop an emergency plan for an earthquake or other natural disaster, take a self-defense class, learn how to screen a person for abuse (that is, how to assess new people you become close to), or make a list of friends you can turn to or stay with when you need support. Even if the dreaded event never happens—or never happens again—having a plan and more knowledge about what's best to do in the situation will put your mind at ease.
2. Let your body know that you have a plan. How do you do this? By letting yourself feel the sensations

that emerge as you review strategies. For example, do you feel lighter? Have your shoulders relaxed? If not, this might be an indication that you need additional resources in place. Maybe you need to know that your pets will be okay in an earthquake. Put together a survival kit of food and water. Organize who would adopt them if something happened to you. Go over your list until you feel it is complete.
3. When your negative thoughts return, tell yourself you have a plan in place, that you thought carefully about each situation, and that this is as much as you can do at this time. Realize that you are again giving emphasis to something you *don't* want to happen, and try to shift your mind away from that and focus instead on what you *do* want to happen.

Belief: I Am Not Worthy

Beliefs such as I am not worthy, I am lesser than, or I am not enough are common among people with low self-esteem. These beliefs are even stronger and more debilitating for people who have experienced being shamed, humiliated, belittled, or dehumanized, which is typical with racism, sexism, homophobia, other forms of discrimination, bullying, verbal abuse, harassment, or any other type of abuse. This was true for my client Jeff, although it was not obvious at first.

When Jeff came to my office, he told me that he was damaging his own success everywhere in his life, including his health. He wanted to lose weight and had attempted this goal many times. Although he knew good steps to losing weight—and would start to take them—he wouldn't carry them through. He hired a trainer, ate healthy and even lost a little weight. When he was starting to arrive closer to his vision, he started drinking beer, eating poorly, canceling his appointments with his trainer, and finding other obstacles to put in his way. This wasn't the only place he sabotaged his success. He told me, "It follows me everywhere, from work to relationships and anywhere else."

After asking him a few questions, I learned that Jeff had been bullied for five years when he was young for being chubby. Jeff's bully, who was an athlete at the time, teased and humiliated him mercilessly, making Jeff think and feel he was lesser than and worthless. Jeff tried to be an athlete and signed up for hockey—he wanted to be like the popular athlete and prove himself—but athletics just weren't him. His strength was his amazing intellect, but nobody pointed that out to him. Nor did anyone notice that he was being bullied or his sadness.

Jeff tried to be someone he was not and failed. There was still a fourth grader in Jeff who believed that he was inferior, that he had to become someone else to be worthy but that his attempts to do so would always fail. From that point on, his coping mechanism was to sabotage everything beforehand so that he wouldn't continue to fail. In therapy, Jeff became aware that he needed to make sure that his current goals reflected who he was and not who he thought he should be—or who he thought he should be when he was young. Now he can take the steps necessary to get where *he* wants to be.

Everyone has a different reason for why they feel unworthy, why they sabotage success, and why they behave the way they do. We have to consider the time when beliefs were formed: a fourth grader will make sense of the world a lot differently than a fifteen-year-old or an adult does. However, the fourth grader's beliefs may never have been modified. They may have been carried into the present moment from a younger, more impressionable, more vulnerable time. The effort to cover up or forget painful parts of our past can contribute to unknowingly carrying old, useless beliefs. We may not be aware that our beliefs are well past their expiration date. However, when you become aware of your beliefs and how they no longer serve you, you can start to create new, positive beliefs that do. Pretty soon you'll notice outward circumstances changing as well.

It's no wonder that a child's self-concept (what we think about ourselves) and self-esteem (how we value ourselves) can be lowered by being bullied and abuse. Self-esteem is how we evaluate ourselves, how we judge if we like what we see about ourselves. With low self-esteem, feeling worthy, powerful, valuable, likable, and successful are often missing from that picture or only partly present.

There's a notion that self-esteem can be a bad thing—this confuses self-esteem with vanity, egotism, or narcissism. High self-esteem is healthy. Narcissism is a different thing altogether. Narcissism is a mental disorder in which people feel superior to others and believe they're entitled to be treated better than others. A narcissist lacks empathy and therefore has a hard time relating to other people: everything is always about the narcissist. But nowhere in any definition of self-esteem does a person with healthy self-esteem lack empathy, compassion, moral values, or a grip on reality. Self-esteem isn't about believing that you are 100 percent perfect.

Someone with healthy self-esteem can reflect on how they can improve; the narcissist with an unhealthy ego lacks that skill. That said, disapproving of or not believing in yourself can certainly make it more difficult to succeed in anything, from relationships to careers and other areas of your life. Please be proud of every step you take toward growth, no matter the outcome; from each step you learn and grow.

Increasing your sense of self-worth can allow you to feel that you deserve happiness and prevent you from sabotaging yourself. The following exercise can help you increase your feeling of being worthy—because you are.

Gain a Sense of Self-Worth

- Every night, write down two things that you appreciate about you or what you did that day. You may want to buy a special notebook for this.
- When you put yourself down, reframe your self-criticism. For example, if you tell yourself that

you aren't smart, try to reverse that thought and feeling. Say, "I *am* smart. I may not know how to do this yet, but I can learn it."
- Do an activity you enjoy and notice the progress you make at it, no matter how small. For example, can you already play the beginning of a tune on the instrument you are learning to play, or did you perhaps exercise five more minutes than usual?
- Join a group of interest. Sharing with people who have the same interest can feel good because we feel we belong. Groups of interest can help us find people we like; bring us validation for knowing, sharing, and gaining information; and offer witnesses for our achievements and goal-setting.

Belief: I Don't Know What I Want

Hanna couldn't figure out what career to pursue and felt stuck. Working with her, I found that whenever I offered a suggestion that could help her, or noted that she appeared to be doing much better, she would become very upset and even angry with me. After I brought this to her attention, she realized that she had trouble allowing herself to want anything or even letting herself be "normal." She explained, "I wish I could allow myself to want so I can figure out what that is." Her deep-seated subconscious belief that she shouldn't want anything prevented her from knowing what she *did* want. Because she wouldn't let herself explore what she wanted, she couldn't figure out what it was. This was confusing to Hanna and may be perplexing to you as you read this as well. Our psyche is complex. What kept Hanna from moving forward—in choosing a career and anything else that could make her happy—wasn't her belief that she didn't know what she wanted, it was not *allowing* herself to know. Wanting is a necessary ingredient for success: you can't reach a goal if you can't give yourself permission to want it.

As we explored where her belief was coming from, Hanna realized that her mother, a medical researcher, was so focused on finding a cure for a terminal disease that Hanna's needs weren't important to her, because she "wasn't dying." Hanna's family was wealthy, and from the outside she seemed to have everything she needed. Her mother didn't realize that Hanna wasn't receiving enough attention and love. Whenever Hanna wanted anything, her mother made her feel the needs of others were always more urgent. As a result, Hanna internalized the idea that she couldn't allow herself to want anything because her needs weren't as important as other people's.

Alexis was neglected as a young child as well. Her mother, who had a terminal disease, slowly died in front of her eyes. Her father became too overwhelmed to deal with the situation and emotionally neglected her. Alexis, too, learned that everyone else's needs came first. As an adult, Alexis had a hard time believing that she deserved to want and have her wants met. Alexis operated her own business. However, she found invoicing her clients very uncomfortable as it brought up both seeming needy (wanting money) and receiving something (getting a check). Even when clients reminded her to tell them how much they owed her, Alexis was afraid to send the invoices. It was only with extreme reluctance that she eventually got paid.

It may feel unfamiliar or wrong to want. Or maybe you feel guilty for what you have. Let me assure you: you have the right to be happy and to receive what you want (without harming others, of course). When you keep yourself from the feeling of wanting, you start to forget what you want and how to want. If you don't know what you like or want in life, use the following exercise to learn your body's clues—your body can tell your mind.

Learn to Recognize What You Want

1. Think of something you know for sure that you *don't* like; this could be a food, a movie, a person, anything.
2. Observe how your body reacts. How do you know that you do not like it? Do you feel tightness,

headache, heaviness, something else? Your discomfort helps you narrow down options by showing you what you don't like.
3. Now, what do you know that you *do* like? Perhaps you like a certain food, going to the beach, hiking in the mountains, or something else. How does your body react when you visualize this? Do you feel an expansion or lightness? Do you smile? Something else? Take some time to focus on these feelings. Let them flower and tell you what your body wants or needs.

***

Keep practicing. As you get better, you'll notice subtleties in your reactions, in both your attractions and your aversions. This type of self-examination will help you get to know your inner world. When you know yourself well, you can trust your intuition and choices more deeply.

Discover and Update Your Outdated Beliefs

We are supposed to learn from our experiences, good ones and bad ones. The beliefs we build from experiences are stored in our subconscious—it's not your fault if some of these beliefs are negative or disempowering. However, you don't need to accept all of the beliefs your subconscious feeds you. Try to start questioning beliefs that don't serve you. Are they really true? Disempowering beliefs can arise for many reasons. It's important that you lovingly discover *your* reasons. Rest assured: whatever your history and your beliefs, you can succeed at your goals, but the more you have your beliefs on your side, the easier that is.

Uncovering your beliefs, both conscious and subconscious, and letting go of the ones that are no longer useful can be uncomfortable. It may make you feel as if you are losing your identity—if your entire life is organized around your fears and beliefs, this may make you feel unsafe. Or you may react with anger—at yourself and the world—for having lived like this and carried this pain for so long. You may also have lots of sadness. Vanessa was glad to have identified her beliefs, but she also felt angry that they had shaped her—angry that it felt like her abuser continued to have power over her.

When you identify the core of your fears, you can also develop a strategy to change them. You don't have to be their hostage. It's totally understandable that Vanessa would be angry. Such anger is a healthy response—a natural part of the continuum of grief and recovery that can help motivate you to make positive changes. But try not to use your discovery about yourself as yet another reason to feel powerless, as you were trained to feel if you grew up in an abusive home. Instead, see how your awareness of your beliefs and the processes that make them can empower you to change. Gaining awareness can be emotionally painful at first; in the long run, it will empower you. Without awareness, making changes is difficult if not impossible.

In order to alter your beliefs, I suggest that you become your own anthropologist. Identify what beliefs you carry in your subconscious by investigating which areas are working in your life and which areas are not. Positive outcomes likely build from your positive beliefs, negative ones from your negative beliefs. Since negative beliefs physically distress your body, you may want to try wearing a stress-band monitor to observe your heart rate and stress level. Some stress bands have additional functions, such as replicating breathing rhythms to help you calm down. Being an observer of your beliefs can help you to distance yourself from them—and thus give you more control over whether or not you want to react to them. The more you inspect your disempowering beliefs, the more chances you have to intervene in negative emotions and actions that hinder you from being successful.

Therefore, *today* is an important day—it can be the beginning of the rest of your life. Every today is a day you can learn from yesterday and start again. Remember: when you update an outdated belief system that hinders your achievements, you make space for new possibilities to appear. In fact, the energy of a different belief invites possibility in. You may be pleasantly surprised how outward circumstances change when you make even a small shift inside. Small internal changes can actually be much more powerful than trying to push the world into being the way you want it. That said, the psyche has its own pace; sometimes the psyche needs time to process new stimuli and make changes. Please remember to be kind to yourself and patient.

The following exercise can help you investigate and release disempowering beliefs. My clients really like using a horse as a metaphor to represent beliefs and fears, but you can choose whatever image or metaphor you prefer. Using a metaphor can help you distance yourself from your beliefs. Metaphors are a wonderful tool because they invite your imagination to participate and engage your creative brain. Metaphors can help bring movement to beliefs and thoughts frozen in time and are often used in guided imagery. In addition, steps 4–7 of this exercise draw on Pat Ogden's sensorimotor exercise (2015, 217) to explore the body sensations that accompany your beliefs and fears.

Hold the Reins of Your Beliefs

1. Become your own observer. Notice when you start to think negatively or become pessimistic. Ask yourself: What do I believe that makes me think like that? What am I afraid of? If you're wearing a stress-band monitor, when it shows that your body is experiencing stress, ask yourself what you're thinking or fearing in that moment that might cause this reaction.
2. Name your belief or fear: "My belief/fear is that _____." For example, "My fear is that I make people jealous when I am successful."
3. Now, imagine that the belief comes as a horse (please use whatever metaphor works for you) and that you feel tempted to ride

it. Pause and imagine yourself first looking at the horse and then realizing that if you get on the horse you will have a bumpy, unpleasant ride. If you let the horse pass, you will avoid this rough ride.
4. What emotions does your belief or fear evoke? For example, do you feel apprehension, terror, guilt, shame, embarrassment, sadness, anger, helplessness, anxiety, worry, regret, loneliness, something else?
5. What body sensations accompany your belief as you think about it? Do you feel heavy shoulders, a constricted chest, tingling arms, numbness, achy, short of breath, something else?
6. Do any small body movements occur with your sensations and emotions? These might include, for example, your jaw or lips tightening, hands curling into fists, leaning back or forward, shoulders tensing, muscles twitching, toes curling, etc.

7. Slowly reverse the small body movements that you have control over. For example, relax your jaw or shoulders, open your fist, straighten your posture, uncurl your toes, etc. Notice how you feel as you do this.
8. What would it feel like if you didn't have this belief? How might parts of your life change? Take a deep breath with this positive thought.
9. Now, decide if you want to ride the horse or let the horse—and its fears—pass.
10. Next time when the negative belief or fear chimes in, tell yourself, "Oh, there's that horse again. I'm not willing to give in to a belief that doesn't serve me. I don't want to go on that unpleasant ride." Try it on—if this sentence doesn't work for you, reframe it as you wish.

Becoming aware of disempowering beliefs requires repetition. So does building the habit of letting go of disempowering beliefs. The more often you practice, the less often negative beliefs and thoughts will interfere.

Conclusion: From Limiting Beliefs to Unlimited Possibilities

Traumatic events can shatter our positive beliefs and challenge how we see the world from that point on, from the present well into the future. The limiting beliefs that result may still be your "truth," even if they are outdated and incorrectly inform and guide you today. Our current thoughts, behavior, emotions, and feelings may be reactions to past experiences and trauma, and not the present. When we investigate which thoughts and feelings tell us the truth and which ones don't, we can begin to disengage from disempowering thoughts and feelings and work on building healthier ones.

Unfortunately, we can think positively all we want with the conscious mind, but our subconscious with its negative beliefs is powerful and usually wins (Lipton 2008). In order to change disempowering beliefs of the past, our affirmations need to be in sync. For example, telling yourself you are worthy may not work unless you have also identified and understood the opposing beliefs in your subconscious. The less limiting your beliefs become—the less you have to swim against the current to reach your goals—the more you can step into the possibilities of your positive conscious mind. While your beliefs after trauma may seem debilitating at first, they *can* lead to new awareness and appreciation for life. Seeing things differently after trauma can ultimately lead to a more meaningful life. Encouraging such posttraumatic growth (Calhoun and Tedeschi 2006) is the subject of the next chapter.

CHAPTER 8

Vuja De: Finding Meaning after Trauma

"The way you look at things is the most powerful force in your life."
—John O'Donohue

Have you started to look at familiar fears, feelings, and behaviors differently now that you realize they may stem from your trauma and not always convey the full truth? If so, you may have had a *vuja de* moment. Comedian George Carlin coined the term *"vuja de"* to mean the opposite of the French idiom *déjà vu* (Bailey 2012). *Déjà vu* literally means "already seen" and conveys an inexplicable feeling of familiarity, as if the moment being experienced has already happened. *"Vuja de,"* in contrast, describes experiencing something familiar as if it were strange and unknown. This can happen, for example, when you suddenly understand a certain feeling or situation entirely differently.

This new lens can bring clarity to your personal story and catalyze changes in your circumstances. New, positive meaning may flow into your life. These new feelings and possibilities can be both exciting and frightening because they are unfamiliar. You may feel confused by this new reference point. You may experience grief and anger—at yourself or others—because you were trapped in the old ways for so long. Stay with your growing confidence and your openness to healing, and continue to overcome your tired old limiting beliefs. As you do, negative reactions can and usually will transform into positive connections with yourself and the people around you, creating conditions for more peace within. You have the opportunity—now and always—to explore and take on new ways of feeling and being, and to find different aspects of meaningfulness in life as a result.

Everything in our lives—events, people, places—offers the opportunity to gain awareness and advance our personal growth. Both through living with and working with your traumatic experiences, you have already come a long way, at times under extremely adverse circumstances. In addition to courage and endurance, healing and recovery require a number of qualities that you may have gained in the process of suffering: wisdom, strength, resilience, humility, and much more. Don't get me wrong: I'm not saying that trauma is "good" for anyone. Rather, I am noting that we can derive value from many experiences by assimilating them. In my own case, if not for my efforts to heal from trauma's effects, I wouldn't have taken the path in life that I did, personally or professionally. It is a journey I would not have gone on otherwise.

This chapter offers my concluding words of encouragement on your journey. I hope to have conveyed that, even though you may have struggled a great deal and may not know when your suffering will end, your life can turn around for the better. Some people find new meaning in life after surviving a traumatic accident, natural disaster, or near-death experience. Others have deep realizations when they are chronically or acutely ill. Some people find meaning only after struggling with the impact of trauma and consciously trying to heal for some time. This search for meaning and healing often continues as we strive to understand life's mysteries and our own ways of being.

Know that, as a result of your journey to heal from trauma, you can gain greater awareness, more love and appreciation for life, a spiritual connection, and an improved approach and outcome to life. This chapter offers ideas for how to help others on their path of healing—which can feel empowering and healing in itself—and concludes with a final meditation exercise to facilitate feelings of inner peace.

Trauma Turned Around: Posttraumatic Growth

Struggling with trauma symptoms is extremely difficult, more so than anyone without this burden can imagine. Research shows that even the most severe traumatic experiences can also be the catalyst for positive changes (e.g., Tedeschi and Calhoun 1996). Adam Jackson's book *The Flipside: Finding the Hidden Opportunities in Life* (2009) features many examples of people turning trauma into personal and spiritual growth. Researchers have found that trying to find meaning after trauma can lead survivors to new understandings of themselves, "about who they are, what people around them are like, what kind of world they live in, or what the future may hold" (Tedeschi and Calhoun 1996, 506), a process called "posttraumatic growth." For example, one study found that survivors of cruise ship disasters self-reported a new approach to life that helped them no longer take life for granted (Joseph 2011, 9).

Notably, posttraumatic growth doesn't happen overnight—and doesn't mean that all trauma symptoms have been permanently eradicated. Posttraumatic growth involves gaining a fresh perspective, inner strength, new opportunities, more appreciation, and/or a new spiritual connection during or after your healing journey (Calhoun and Tedeschi 2006). I've observed in my practice that it also often includes greater compassion and love for others as well.

In his book, *Man's Search for Meaning,* Holocaust survivor Victor Frankl (2006) describes how those who were able to find some kind of meaning to hold onto while in the concentration camp were able to stay sane and somehow endure the daily torture. For Frankl, this was his love for his wife. Thoughts of reuniting with his wife gave him meaning and strength when it seemed impossible to keep living and enduring the pain.

Another famous example of posttraumatic growth is Oprah Winfrey, who had a difficult childhood, experiencing poverty, physical and sexual abuse, and neglect (Winfrey 2014). Trauma did not hold her back—as an adult she became a supremely successful businessperson, entertainer, and philanthropist, famous both for being the richest African

American in the world and a compassionate person. The lessons she built out of her experiences gave impetus to her many talents that in turn led to her talk show, acting career, and media empire, as well as a book called *What I Know for Sure* in which she shares some of her stories.

My client Alyssa explained that, after she lost her home and all her belongings in a fire, she gained a new perspective in life and learned to accept help and freshly appreciate her friends and community. Previously, she had never asked for help, and she was continually amazed at how much it brought to her life to open up to this aspect of community and self.

As detailed in his personal account, *The Cancer Code,* when Mike Jetter was diagnosed with leukemia, he focused on his creativity during the three months of isolation his treatment required—and invented a mind-mapping software product called Mindjet, which turned into a million-dollar company (Jetter and Jetter 2003).

For Michael, whom we've met throughout these pages, the suffering he experienced as a child and young adult motivated him to become a doctor and help others. After a great deal of work to overcome his trauma, Michael found himself feeling compassion for his parents and the people who hurt him. He doesn't hold any grudges toward his father or his abusive babysitter.

As for myself, my traumatic experiences led me to grow new opportunities by studying psychology and various healing modalities, to become a psychotherapist, to give workshops, and to write a blog as well as this book.

These are not rare cases. For example, one study found that 58 percent of 9/11 survivors experienced some kind of positive change over the subsequent three years (Joseph 2011). The positive change of posttraumatic growth can take a number of forms, including finding a new and useful life philosophy, a new awareness of your strengths, clarity about your direction in life, appreciation and gratitude for your blessings, and love for life, others, and yourself. For some people, posttraumatic growth can go beyond emotional and physical wellbeing to seeking—and finding—a rewarding and joyful spiritual connection (Tedeschi and Calhoun 2009).

A Spiritual Connection

Spiritual connections don't have to be otherworldly or miraculous. A spiritual connection can be as simple, for example, as a peaceful and calm feeling accompanied by a heightened awareness of being. Spiritual feelings can also emerge when you finally feel connected again to life and love after a long period of feeling disconnected due to trauma. Sometimes, surviving a life-threatening event can prompt a spiritual viewpoint, such as feeling that fate or a higher power saved you or making you grateful for every moment of life you are subsequently "gifted" with.

Faith can be lost, created, or strengthened by trauma. After trauma, some trauma survivors have a stronger faith than ever. Others find their faith decimated by extreme misfortune or circumstances. Yet others become spiritual seekers.

Belief in a higher power and having a spiritual community can serve as key support systems for coping with trauma and its aftermath. One study found that 92 percent of Hurricane Katrina survivors who were evacuated to shelters in Houston said that their faith played an important role in helping them get through the ordeal (Kaiser Family Foundation 2005). Trauma tends to cause us to focus on our emotional and physical pain and can bring about isolation. A spiritual community can help turn our attention away from our pain and connect us back to the world around us. (As I discuss in the next section, this also applies to nonspiritual communities of friends and neighbors and family.) Connecting to a world that is perceived as more wholesome or about unconditional love and forgiveness can help bridge the loss of safety and rupture of love that trauma causes. Ideally, a spiritual community will be nonjudgmental and loving. Faith can also provide strength when you feel like you want to lean on someone or something stronger, bringing hope to a hopeless state.

Unfortunately, people searching for love, connection, and meaning in life may sometimes encounter people or systems that will use their power and authority to exploit or abuse others who are vulnerable. Prominent figures in religious and spiritual life are not excluded. Countless people have been abused by religious and spiritual leaders. In 2002, investigations by the *Boston Globe* exposed systemic covering up of child sex abuse by Catholic priests, portrayed in the movie *Spotlight.* The founder of Bikram yoga, Bikram Choudhury, and Swami Akhandananda, a spiritual leader of Mangrove Yoga Ashram, are two other examples of abusive, formerly respected spiritual leaders.

Having a spiritual connection doesn't necessitate trusting a self-proclaimed or appointed religious figure. You can create your own spirituality. Spirituality can be found in the beauty and wholeness of the natural world, a good hike, a fun time, a great work of art, or inside yourself. When I asked my client Laura, who was in an abusive marriage, what spirituality meant to her, she said, "How can I possibly describe this? I began to have a sense inside of myself of what was right and what was wrong—what felt like the right direction." Her new direction—which included getting a divorce from her abusive husband even though she loved him, selling her house, making new friends, and following her newly found self—helped Laura to see her path with greater clarity and wisdom. She continued, "I know this doesn't sound spiritual, but to me it is." Everyone has their own personal definition of spirituality and their own path to finding meaning. It's important to allow yourself to experience this.

Community Support Makes a Difference

Kindness from others can make a difference in anyone's life. Not surprisingly, studies have shown that receiving support from others can reduce the development of trauma symptoms (Joseph 2011; Ozbay et al.

2007) and help foster posttraumatic growth (Meichenbaum 2006). Both active and moral support from a trauma survivor's community may help survivors feel they are not forgotten (van der Kolk 2011) and provide comfort. In cases of natural disaster, caring gestures can include expressing emotional support, signing up for volunteer work, donating blood, or donating needed materials or money. In addition to benefiting directly from the help of others, just knowing about such help can encourage survivors and help them summon the strength and motivation to overcome traumatic events and trauma symptoms.

Michael highlighted that even having just one person who cares can make a difference to an abused child. If it were not for Michael's teacher Mrs. Sullivan, who showed that she understood and cared about him when he was growing up, he would have been in a much worse state than he was. "Mrs. Sullivan was my savior," Michael recalled. "She really did love me."

While a single person can make a huge difference in an abused child's life, a community can have an even greater impact. Stopping abuse from happening, whether that's at home, school, in church, or anywhere else, is a difficult, ongoing battle. That said, there are ways to reduce abuse right now. A key one is education. Abuse survivors as well as abusers themselves need to be made aware of and recognize what abuse is so that the survivors can look for appropriate resources and receive help, and the abusers can recognize what they are doing to seek assistance to stop it. More than that, our community members—including parents, teachers, health and mental health care providers, priests, EVERYONE—need to learn about abuse so that they can recognize it and initiate help.

We cannot be bystanders. Repairing and widening interpersonal connections is a fundamental part of trauma recovery (Herman 2015). Advocating for survivors, as well as providing support and education, can make a difference. Ideally we would have trained professionals in our schools, at work, church, and elsewhere, to watch for signs of abuse. Such professionals could provide resources to educate, treat, and counsel, and take other appropriate and constructive actions.

Helping others—such as by spreading the words and techniques in this book—can both reduce abuse and help you, too. Last but not least: Try to be kind to those around you. They may just suffer from trauma and have no other way of being right now.

Our final exercise draws on Herbert Benson's (2000) work on relaxation. As, Benson, a professor at Harvard Medical School, describes in his book *The Relaxation Response,* when the mind is focused for 10 to 20 minutes, the body responds by relaxing, thus counteracting the flight–fight–freeze response. The relaxation response can be accomplished in a variety of ways, including chanting, sitting quietly and focusing on the breath, workouts, and morning strolls. I think of this as "meditation on the go," because you don't have to be sitting at home to practice it.

Meditation isn't only for Buddhists or yogis—it's for anyone who wants to experience a peaceful mind and better focus in all daily activities. Meditation aims to train the mind to release thoughts that do not serve you; to let the mind recognize the thoughts you have without attaching to them; and to find peace of mind and calmness. The following exercise can help you with this.

Meditation on the Go

Choose whether you want to practice the relaxation response sitting quietly and meditating or while actively praying, jogging, swimming, walking, or doing any other activity.

For 10 to 20 minutes, practice repeating a mantra, prayer, words, or sounds out loud or in your head. You can also repeat a movement or look at something soothing or comforting for this time frame. Pay attention to your pace, rhythm, breath, or anything else you are drawn to. Observe your feelings and sensations. If your mind starts to chatter, just notice what you are thinking about and go back to repeating sounds, words, phrases, or prayers.

After focusing for 10 to 20 minutes, when you feel calm and your mind is settled, envision the outcome you would like to have. This will help you rewire your thoughts. If you have a hard time visualizing desired outcomes on your own, find some pictures online or in a magazine and create a collage or vision board. Place this in front of you to help you visualize.

The relaxation response can restore calmness, a state that many trauma survivors have lost access to. Further, it works as a simple, helpful coping mechanism in stressful and traumatic situations.

Conclusion: From Breakdown to Breakthrough

Trauma may have brought you to your knees, but your healing journey has ultimately led you—or can lead you—to a better place you never imagined you'd be. Even if you are not there yet, you have a very good chance of getting there. Keep going and don't give up.

References

Ainsworth, M. and J. Bowlby. 1965. *Child Care and the Growth of Love.* London: Penguin Books.

Ainsworth, M.D.S., M.C. Blehar, E. Walters, and S. Wall. 2015. *Patterns of Attachment: A Psychological Study of the Strange Situation.* New York: Psychology Press.

American Psychiatric Association. 2013. *The Diagnostic and Statistical Manual of Mental Disorders, DSM-V.* Arlington, VA: American Psychiatric Association.

Ardiel, E.L., and C.H. Rankin. 2010. "The Importance of Touch in Development." *Paediatrics Child Health* 15: 153–156.

Arnett, J.J. 2010. *Adolescence and Emerging Adulthood.* Upper Saddle River, NJ: Prentice Hall/Pearson.

Aronson, E., T.D. Wilson, and R.M. Akert. 2011. *Social Psychology.* 7th ed.

Upper Saddle River, NJ: Prentice Hall/Pearson.

Babbel, S. 2007. *Compassion Fatigue: A Heuristic Study of Somatic Psychotherapists Treating Traumatized Clients.* Santa Barbara, CA: Santa Barbara Graduate Institute.

Bailey, S.T. 2012. *The Vujá dé Moment: Shift from Average to Brilliant.* Windermere, FL: Dream Tree Productions.

Baz, B., and N.E. Wang. 2013. "Physical Abuse of Children: Identification, Evaluation, and Management in the ED Setting." Pediatric Emergency Medicine Reports. http://www.ahcmedia.com/articles/30973-physical-abuse-of-children-identification-evaluation-and-management. Accessed June 2016.

Beckham, E., and C. Beckham. 2004. "A Personal Guide to Coping." *Coping with Negative Thinking.* http://docplayer.net/1790131-Coping-with-trauma-and-post-traumatic-stress-disorder-ed-bec kham-ph-d-and-cecilia-beckham-l-c-s-w-bc-d.html. Accessed May 2015.

Benson, H. 2000. *The Relaxation Response.* New York: Harper Collins Publishers.

Boscarino, J.A. 2004. "Posttraumatic Stress Disorder and Physical Illness: Results from Clinical and Epidemiologic Studies." *Annals of the New York Academy of Sciences* 1032: 141–153.

Bowen, M. 1966. "The Use of Family Theory in Clinical Practice." *Comprehensive Psychiatry* 7: 345–374.

Bowlby, J. 1951. "Maternal Care and Mental Health." *Bulletin of the World Health Organization. Geneva: World Health Organization* 3: 355–533.

Bowlby, J. 1960. "Separation Anxiety." *International Journal of Psychoanalysis* 41: 89–113.

Bowlby, J. 1969. *Attachment & Loss, Volume 1, Attachment.* New York: Basic Books.

Bremner, J.D., J.H. Krystal, S.M. Southwick, and D.S. Charney. 1996. "Noradrenergic Mechanisms in Stress and Anxiety: II Clinical Studies." *Synapse* 23: 39–51.

Brown, B. 2010. "The Power of Vulnerability." TED talk. Posted June 2010. 20 min. http://www.ted.com/talks/brene_brown_on_vulnerability/transcript?language=en

Calhoun, L.G., and R.G. Tedeschi. 2006. *Handbook of Posttraumatic Growth: Research and Practice.* Abingdon, UK: Routledge.

Cann, A., L.G. Calhoun, R.G. Tedeschi, K. Taku, T. Vishnevsky, K.N. Triplett, and S.C. Danhauer. 2010. "A Short Form of the Posttraumatic Growth Inventory." *Anxiety, Stress & Coping* 23:127–137.

Carney, D.R., A.J.C. Cuddy, and A.J. Yap. J. 2010. "Power Posing: Brief Nonverbal Displays Affect Neuroendocrine Levels and Risk

Tolerance." *Psychological Science* 21: 1363–1368.

Chamberlain, D.B. 1988. *Babies Remember Birth: And Other Extraordinary Scientific Discoveries About the Mind and Personality of Your Newborn.* New York: Jeremy P. Tarcher, Inc.

Cheek, D.B. 1986. "Prenatal and Perinatal Imprints: Apparent Prenatal Consciousness as Revealed by Hypnosis." *Journal of Prenatal & Perinatal Psychology & Health* 1: 97–110.

Cohen, H., L. Neumann, Y. Haiman, M.A. Matar, J. Press, and D. Buskila. 2002. "Prevalence of Post-Traumatic Stress Disorder in Fibromyalgia Patients: Overlapping Syndromes or Post-Traumatic Fibromyalgia Syndrome?" *Seminars in Arthritis and Rheumatism* 32: 38–50.

Cox, K.S., H.S. Resnick, and D.G. Kilpatrick. 2014. "Prevalence and Correlates Posttrauma Distorted Beliefs:

Evaluating DSM-5 PTSD Expanded Cognitive Symptoms in a National Sample." *Journal of Traumatic Stress* 27: 299–306.

Craig, G. 2009. *EFT for PTSD (EFT: Emotional Freedom Technique).* Fulton, CA: Energy Psychology Press.

Davila, J., D. Burge, and C. Hammen. 1997. "Why Does Attachment Style Change?" *Journal of Personality and Social Psychology* 73: 826–838.

Davis, L. 2002. *I Thought We'd Never Speak Again: The Road from Estrangement to Reconciliation.* New York: Harper Collins Publishing.

Defrin, R., K. Ginzburg, Z. Solomon, E. Polad, M. Bloch, M. Govezensky, and S. Schreiber. 2008. "Quantitative Testing of Pain Perception in Subjects with PTSD—Implications for the Mechanism of the Coexistence Between PTSD and Chronic Pain." *Pain* 138: 450–459.

DeSilva, P. 1999. "Sexual Consequences of Non-sexual Trauma." *Sexual and Marital Therapy* 14: 143–155.

Ehlers, A., and D.M. Clark. 2000. "A Cognitive Model of Posttraumatic Stress Disorder." *Behaviour Research & Therapy,* 38: 319–345.

Evans, P. 2003. *Controlling People: How to Recognize, Understand and Deal with People Who Try to Control You.* Avon, MA: Adams Media Corporation.

Figley, C.R. 2002. "Compassion Fatigue: Psychotherapists' Chronic Lack of Self Care." *Journal of Clinical Psychology,* 58(11): 1433–1441.

Finkelhor, D., and A. Browne. 1985. "The Traumatic Impact of Child Sexual Abuse: A Conceptualization." *American Journal of Orthopsychiatry* 55: 530–541.

Firestone, R.W., and J. Cattlett. 2009. *The Ethics of Interpersonal Relationships.* London: Karnac Books.

Ford, J.D., and E. Russo. 2006. "Trauma-Focused, Present-Centered, Emotional Self-Regulation Approach to Integrated Treatment for Posttraumatic Stress and Addiction: Trauma Adaptive Recovery Group Education and Therapy (TARGET)." *American Journal of Psychotherapy* 60: 335–355.

Frankl, V.E., and W.J. Winslade. 2006. *Man's Search for Meaning.* Boston: Beacon Press.

Galinsky, A.D., D.H. Gruenfeld, and J.C. Magee. 2003. "From Power to Action." *Journal of Personality and Social Psychology* 85: 453–466.

Garbinsky, E.N., A. Klesse, and A. Jennifer. 2014. "Money in the Bank: Feeling Powerful Increases Saving." *Journal of Consumer Research* 41(3): 610–623.

Goldsmith, M. 2015. *Triggers: Sparking Positive Change and Making It Last.* New York: Random House, Inc.

Gonzalez-Gonzalez, N.L., M.N. Suarez, B. Perez-Pinero, H. Armas, E. Domenech, and J.L. Bartha. 2006. "Persistence of Fetal Memory into Neonatal Life." *Acta Obstetricia et Gynecologica Scandinavica* 85: 1160–1164.

Goulston, M. 2008. *Post-Traumatic Stress Disorder for Dummies.* Hoboken, NJ: Wiley Publishing.

Hanna, T. 2003. "What Is Somatics?" *Journal of the Mind/Body Arts and Sciences* 14(2): 50–55.

Hazan, C., and P. Shaver. 1987. "Romantic Love Conceptualized as an Attachment Process." *Journal of Personality and Social Psychology* 52: 511–524.

Hendricks, G., and K. Hendricks. 1991. *Radiance: Breathwork, Movement and Body-Centered Psychotherapy.* Godalming, UK: Bookpeople.

Helgeson, V.S., K.A. Reynolds, and P.L. Tomich. 2006. "A Meta-analytic Review of Benefit Finding and Growth." *Journal of Consulting and Clinical Psychology* 74: 797–816.

Herman, J. 2015. *Trauma and Recovery: The Aftermath of Violence—From Domestic Abuse to Political Terror.* New York: Basic Books.

Hughes, C., S.L. Lusk, and S. Strause. 2016. "Recognizing and Accommodating Employees with PTSD: The Intersection of Human Resource Development, Rehabilitation, and Psychology." *New Horizons in Adult Education & Human Resource Development* 28: 27–39.

Jackson, A. 2009. *The Flipside: Finding the Hidden Opportunities in Life.* London: Headline Book Publishing.

Jacobs, G.D. 2001. "The Physiology of Mind-Body Interactions: The Stress Response and the Relaxation Response." *The Journal of Alternative and Complementary Medicine.* 7: 83–92.

Jacobson, E. 1946. *Progressive Relaxation: A Physiological and Clinical Investigation of Muscular States and their Significance in Psychology and Medical Practice.* Chicago: University of Chicago Press.

Janus, L. 1997. *The Enduring Effects of Prenatal Experience: Echoes from the Womb.* Northvale, NJ: Jason Aronson, Inc.

Jetter, M., and B. Jetter. 2003. *The Cancer Code: How a Journey through Leukemia Led to Software that Changed the Way People Work.* Self-published.

Joseph, S. 2011. *What Doesn't Kill Us: A New Psychology of Posttraumatic Growth.* New York: Basic Books.

Joseph, J.S., and M.J. Gray. 2008. "Exposure Therapy for Posttraumatic Stress Disorder." *The Journal of Behavior Analysis of Offender and Victim Treatment and Prevention* 1(4): 69–79.

Kaiser Family Foundation. 2005. "Survey of Hurricane Katrina Evacuees." Posted August 31. http://www.kff.org/disparities-policy/report/survey-of-hurricane-katrina-evacuees/. Accessed July 2017.

Katz, D.A., and C. McHorney. 2002. "The Relationship Between Insomnia and Health-Related Quality of Life in Patients With Chronic Illness." *The Journal of Family Practice* 51: 229–235.

Kazdin, A. 2009. *The Kazdin Method for Parenting the Defiant Child.* New York: Houghton Mifflin Harcourt Publishing Company.

Keesling, B. 2006. *Sexual Healing: A Complete Guide To Overcoming Common Sexual Problems.* Alameda, CA: Hunter House Inc.

Keleman, S. 1981. *Your Body Speaks Its Mind.* Westlake Village, CA: Center Press.

Klontz, B., and T. Klontz. 2009. *Mind Over Money. Overcoming the Money*

Disorders that Threaten Our Financial Health. New York: Random House.

Kübler-Ross, E., and D. Kessler. 2007. *On Grief and Grieving: Finding the Meaning of Grief Through the Five Stages of Loss.* New York: Scribner.

Levine, A., and R.S.F. Heller. 2011. *Attached: The New Science of Adult Attachment and How It Can Help You Find and Keep Love.* New York: Penguin Group.

Levine, P.A. 2005, 2008. *Healing Trauma.* Louisville, CO: Sounds True, Inc.

Levine, P.A. 2010. *In an Unspoken Voice: How the Body Releases Trauma and Restores Goodness.* Berkeley, CA: North Atlantic Books.

Levine, P.A. 1997. *Waking the Tiger.* Berkeley, CA: North Atlantic Books.

Lipton, B. 2008. *The Biology of Belief.* Carlsbad, CA: Hay House.

Lloyd, E. 2006. *The Case of the Female Orgasm.* Cambridge, MA: Harvard University Press.

MacDonald, H.A., V. Colotla, S. Flamer, and H. Karlinsky. 2003. "Posttraumatic Stress Disorder (PTSD) in the Workplace: A Descriptive Study of Workers Experiencing PTSD Resulting from Work Injury." *Journal of Occupational Rehabilitation* 13: 63–77.

Mandela, N. 1995. *Long Walk to Freedom.* New York: Back Bay Books.

Marshall, A.N. 2012. "A Clinician's Guide to Recognizing and Reporting Parental Psychological Maltreatment of Children." *Professional Psychology: Research and Practice* 43: 73–79.

Maslow, A.H. 1943. "A Theory of Human Motivation." *Psychological Review* 50(4): 370–396.

Maslow, A.H. 1954. *Motivation and Personality.* New York: Harper and Row.

Maurer, R. 2004. *One Small Step Can Change Your Life: The Kaizen Way.* New York: Workman Publishing Company.

Meichenbaum, D. 2006. "Resilience and Posttraumatic Growth: A Constructive Narrative Perspective." In *Handbook of Posttraumatic Growth: Research and Practice,* edited by L.G. Calhoun and R.G. Tedeschi. Abingdon, UK: Routledge.

Mills, B.C.S. 2001. "Editorial. Special Issue: Trauma, Sexuality, and Relationships." *Sexual and Relationship Therapy* 16: 197–205. In Mills, B. and Turnbull, G. 2004. "Broken Hearts and Mending Bodies: The Impact of Trauma on Intimacy." *Sexual and Relationship Therapy* 19: 265–289.

Mills, B., and G. Turnbull. 2004. "Broken Hearts and Mending Bodies: The Impact of Trauma on Intimacy." *Sexual and Relationship Therapy* 19: 265–289.

Nin, Anaïs. 1996. *The Diary of Anaïs Nin.* Santa Barbara, CA: Capra Press.

Northrup, C. 2005. *Mother-Daughter Wisdom.* New York: Bantam Books.

O'Brian, K.L., L. Cohen, J.N. Pooley, and M.F. Taylor. 2012. "Lifting the Domestic Violence Cloak of Silence: Resilient Australian Women's Reflected Memories of their Childhood Experiences of Witnessing Domestic Violence." *Journal of Family Violence* 28: 95–108.

O'Donohue, J. 1998. *Anam Cara: A Book on Celtic Wisdom.* New York, NY; Harper Perennial.

Ogden, P. 2015. *Sensorimotor Psychotherapy: Interventions for Trauma and Attachment.* New York: W.W. Norton & Company, Inc.

Ozbay, F., D.C. Johnson, E. Dimoulas, C.A. Morgan, D. Charney, and S. Southwick. 2007. "Social Support and Resilience to Stress." *Neurobiology to Clinical Practice* 4: 35–40.

Pearlman, L.A., and K.W. Saakvitne. 1996. *Transforming the Pain: A*

Workbook on Vicarious Traumatization. New York: Norton.

Pietromonaco, P.R., and K.B. Carnelley. 1994. "Gender and Working Models of Attachment: Consequences for Perception of Self and Romantic Relationships." *Personal Relationships* 1: 63–82.

Porges, S. 1995. "Orienting in a Defensive World: Mammalian Modifications of Our Evolutionary Heritage. A Polyvagal Theory," *Psychophysiology* 32: 301–318.

Porges, S.W. 2004. "Neuroception: A Subconscious System for Detecting Threats and Safety." *Zero Three* 24: 19–24.

Prather, H., and G. Prather. 2001. *Notes to Each Other.* New York: MJF Books.

Price, C.J., B. McBride, L. Hyerle, and D.R. Kivlahan. 2007. "Mindful Awareness in Body-Oriented Therapy for Female Veterans with Post-Traumatic Stress Disorder taking

Prescription Analgesics for Chronic Pain: A Feasibility Study." *Alternative Therapy in Health and Medicine* 13: 32–40.

Psaris, J., and M.S. Lyons. 2000. *Undefended Love.* Oakland, CA: New Harbinger Publications.

Rand, M.L., and G. Fewster. 2015. "Self, Body, and Boundaries." www.drrandbodymindtherapy.com/self-body-andboundaries. June 3. Accessed June 2016.

Rellini, A., and C. Meston. 2006. "Psychophysiological Sexual Arousal in Women with a History of Childhood Sexual Abuse." *Journal of Sex and Marital Therapy* 32: 5–22.

Rescorla, R.A. 1967. "Pavlovian Conditioning and Its Proper Control Procedures." *Psychological Review* 74: 71–80.

Rogers, C.R. 1959. "A Theory of Therapy, Personality and Interpersonal Relationships as Developed in the Client-Centered Framework." In *Psychology: A Study of a Science.*

Vol.3: Formulations of the Person and the Social Context, edited by S. Koch. New York: McGraw Hill.

Rose, Kathy. 2017. "Prince Harry's Journey of Healing." *The Mountain Astrologer,* Oct-Nov: 48–53.

Rothschild, B. 2000. *The Body Remembers: The Psychophysiology of Trauma and Trauma Treatment.* New York: W.W. Norton & Company.

Rothschild, B. 2006. *Help for the Helper: The Psychophysiology of Compassion Fatigue and Vicarious Traumatization.* New York: W.W. Norton & Company.

Scaer, R. 2014. *The Body Bears the Burden: Trauma, Dissociation, and Disease.* 3rd ed. New York: Routledge.

Schaffer, H.R., and P.E. Emerson. 1964. "The Development of Social Attachments in Infancy." *Monographs of the Society for Research in Child Development* 29: 1–77.

Schnarch, D. 1997. *Passionate Marriage.* New York: Henry Holt and Company.

Scurlock-Durana, S. 2017. *Reclaiming Your Body: Healing from Trauma and Awakening to Your Body's Wisdom.* Novato, CA: New World Library.

Siegel, J.D. 2011. *Mindsight: New Science of Personal Transformation.* New York: Bantam Books.

Siegel, J.D., and M. Solomon. 2003. *Healing Trauma: Attachment, Mind, Body and Brain.* New York: W.W. Norton & Company.

Silverstein, J.L. 1989. "Origins of Psychogenic Vaginismus." *Psychotherapy and Psychosomatics* 52: 197–204.

Skinner, B.F. 1938. *The Behavior of Organisms: An Experimental Analysis.* New York: Appleton-Century.

Smith, B.L. 2012. "The Case Against Spanking." *Monitor on Psychology* 43: 60.

Solomon, Z. 1993. *Combat Stress Reaction: The Enduring Toll of War.* New York: Plenum Publishing Corp.

Stamm, B.H. (ed.). 1999. *Secondary Traumatic Stress: Self Care Issues for Clinicians, Researchers, & Educators,* 2nd edition. Baltimore: Sidran Press.

Szegedy-Maszak, M. 2005. "Mysteries of the Mind: Your Unconscious Is Making Your Everyday Decisions." *U.S. News & World Report,* February 28, 2005.

Taku, K., A. Cann, R.G. Tedeschi, and L.G. Calhoun. 2009. "Intrusive Versus Deliberate Rumination in Posttraumatic Growth Across US and Japanese Samples." *Anxiety, Stress and Coping* 22: 129–136.

Tedeschi, R.G., and L.G. Calhoun. 1996. "The Posttraumatic Growth Inventory: Measuring the Positive Legacy of Trauma." *Journal of Traumatic Stress.* 9(3): 455–471.

Tedeschi, R.G., and L.G. Calhoun. 2009. "Posttraumatic Growth: Conceptual Foundations and Empirical Evidence." *Psychological Inquiry,* 15(1): 1–18.

U.S. Department of Health and Human Services. 2013. "What Is Child Abuse and Neglect? Recognizing the Signs and Symptoms." Child Welfare Information Gateway, https://www.childwelfare.gov/pubpdfs/whatiscan.pdf. Accessed May 13, 2017.

Van der Kolk, B., A.C. McFarlane, and L. Weisach. 1996. *Traumatic Stress: The Effects of Overwhelming Experience on Mind, Body, and Society.* New York: Guilford Press.

Van der Kolk, B. 2011. "New Frontiers in Trauma Treatment," presented at Institute for the Advancement of Human Behavior (IAHB) conference, March 17-18, San Francisco.

Van der Kolk, B. 2014. *The Body Keeps the Score: Brain, Mind, and Body in the Healing of Trauma.* New York: Penguin Books.

Weaver, J. 2004. "The Influence of Elsa Gindler on Somatic Psychotherapy and on Charlotte Selver." *USA Body Psychotherapy Journal* 3(1): 38–47.

Wenzel, A. 2012. "Modification of Core Beliefs in Cognitive Therapy." In *Standard and Innovative Strategies in Cognitive Behavior,* edited by I. Reis de Oliveira. Rijeka, Croatia: InTech. 17–34.

Winfrey, Oprah. 2014. *What I Know For Sure.* New York; Hearst Communications, Inc.

Yehuda, R., A. Lehrer, and T.Y. Rosenbaum. 2015. "PTSD and Sexual Dysfunction in Men and Women." *The Journal of Sexual Medicine* 12: 1107–1119.

Susanne Babbel, PhD, is a licensed psychotherapist with a trauma specialty in private practice in San Francisco, CA. She is a member of the California Association of Marriage and Family Therapists (CAMFT), as well as the United States Association for Body Psychotherapy (USABP) and European Association for Body Psychotherapy (EABP). A contributing author for nearly a decade to the *Psychology Today* online blog, Babbel also writes for magazines and newspapers, appears on radio shows, creates CDs for healing, and co-taught the UC Davis Extension online course on trauma bonding.

Foreword writer **Marti Glenn, PhD,** is cofounder and clinical director of Ryzio Institute, and founding president of Santa Barbara Graduate Institute. She holds degrees in prenatal, perinatal, somatic, and clinical psychology. Glenn served on the board of directors and chaired several Association for Prenatal and Perinatal Psychology and Health (APPPAH) conferences. She coproduced the documentary *Trauma, Brain, and Relationship: Helping Children Heal;* and has appeared in *What Babies Want,*

What Babies Know, and *Reducing Infant Mortality and Improving the Health of Babies.* She conducts training programs and speaks at conferences worldwide.

MORE BOOKS *from* NEW HARBINGER PUBLICATIONS

A MINDFULNESS-BASED STRESS REDUCTION WORKBOOK

BUDDHA'S BRAIN
The Practical Neuroscience of Happiness, Love & Wisdom

MEDITATIONS FOR HEALING TRAUMA
Mindfulness Skills to Ease Post-Traumatic Stress

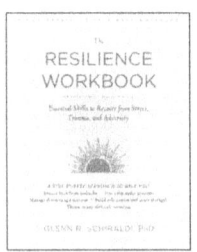

THE RESILIENCE WORKBOOK
Essential Skills to Recover from Stress, Trauma & Adversity

GOODNIGHT MIND
Turn Off Your Noisy Thoughts & Get a Good Night's Sleep

THE UNTETHERED SOUL
The Journey Beyond Yourself

newharbingerpublications
1-800-748-6273 / newharbinger.com

(VISA, MC, AMEX / prices subject to change without notice)

Follow Us

Don't miss out on new books in the subjects that interest you.
Sign up for our Book Alerts at **newharbinger.com/bookalerts**

Back Cover Material

A gentle guide to help you heal from trauma

Trauma can leave both mental *and* physical scars. If you've experienced a traumatic situation—such as the sudden loss of a loved one, a serious illness, abuse, violence, or a natural disaster—you may have ongoing psychological and physiological symptoms. You aren't alone, and you can heal. This book will help you understand how unresolved trauma can infiltrate all aspects of your life, and provides real tools to help you find peace in body and mind.

Heal the Body, Heal the Mind offers somatic exercises and mind-body interventions to help you move past difficult experiences, restore relationships, and even cultivate your own spiritual awareness. Using the exercises woven into each chapter of this gentle guide, you'll begin to address the unresolved trauma held in your body so you can advance your healing process. If you're ready to move beyond the trauma that's been holding you back in life, this book will show you how.

"Comprehensive, thoughtful, well written, and scientifically grounded."
—PETER A. LEVINE, PhD, author of *Waking the Tiger*

"A source of wisdom, empowering readers to break through limitations and achieve their highest potential."
—PATRICIA EVANS, author of *The Verbally Abusive Relationship*

SUSANNE BABBEL, PhD, is a licensed psychotherapist specializing in trauma. She maintains a private practice in San Francisco, CA.

Foreword writer **MARTI GLENN, PhD,** is cofounder and clinical director of Ryzio Institute.

www.ingramcontent.com/pod-product-compliance
Lightning Source LLC
Chambersburg PA
CBHW071315150426
43191CB00007B/633